Branching Out:

Genealogy
Lessons for Adults

Helping You Inspire
The Next Generation

Copyright Information

Publisher: Generations, Woodridge, Illinois

Editor: Stephanie Pitcher Fishman
Cover Designer: Sarah Sucansky, Tree artwork by potatoestomatoes (www.potatoestomatoes.co.uk)

Holik, Jennifer, 1973 –
    Branching Out: Genealogy Lessons for Adults, Helping You Inspire the Next Gneration / Jennifer Holik.

    ISBN 978-1-938226-13-7

This book is dedicated with love to
my three boys: Andrew, Luke, and Tyler Urban. And,
to my good friend and editor, Stephanie Pitcher Fishman. Without
her inspiration this book would not have been written.

Acknowledgments

This series of genealogy lesson books could not have been written without the support of several people. First, I'd like to thank Andrew, Luke, and Tyler Urban, and my best friend, Patti Fleck, for their love and support. The five of you are helping to make my dreams come true!

Thank you to my cousin, Sarah Sucansky, for designing my covers. Thank you to my good friends Stephanie Pitcher Fishman, for editing the books, and Shelley Bishop, Caroline Pointer, Laura Cosgrove Lorenzana and Terri O'Connell for contributing lessons. Thank you to On the Beaton Path (http://onthebeatonpath.com) and Base Zero Productions (http://bzprod.com) for the fabulous new website!

I would also like to thank Debra Dudek of the Fountaindale Public Library in Bolingbrook, IL, and Tony Kierna of the Schaumburg Township District Library, in Schaumburg, IL, for the many times they listened to me talk about the project and offered ideas and encouragement. Also Derek Davey who is associated with the Ohio Genealogical Society for providing feedback about the series.

Introduction

This book is meant to be a starting point for adults wishing to learn the history of their family. It is meant to inspire you to study your families and history in general. At the end of your studies I hope you have a firm foundation of the basics of genealogical research and records. I hope you will continue your research beyond the suggestions in this book. I hope you will be so inspired by your research findings that you will join and become active in a local genealogical or historical society.

Table of Contents

© 2012 Generations, Jennifer Holik

Chpt 3 - flut   Source - Wickey (Ancestry) -
13
13
Next

Items Needed

Most lessons in this book will require the following supplies:
Notebook, Pen or pencil, Three-ring binder, computer.

Required Books:

You may purchase these or obtain through your library.

Croom, Emily Anne. *The Genealogist's Companion and Sourcebook.* Cincinnati: Betterway Books, 2003.

Greenwood, Val D. *The Researcher's Guide to American Genealogy.* Baltimore: Genealogical Publishing Company, 2000.

Mills, Elizabeth Shown. *Evidence Explained Citing History Sources from Artifacts to Cyberspace.* Baltimore: Genealogical Publishing Company, 2009. *Note: This book can be found in most libraries. You will begin using it after lesson seven.

Rose, Christine. *Courthouse Research for Family Historians.* San Jose: CR Publications, 2004.

Szucs, Loretto Dennis, and Luebking, Sandra Hargreaves, eds. *The Source A Guidebook to American Genealogy.* Provo: The Generations Network, 2006. *Note: This book can be found on Ancestry.com's Wiki in full text. URLs are noted in each lesson.

Additional Resources:

These books are not required for this course. They are just additional resources for the parents and teachers, should they like to further their genealogical education or provide other resources for their children. Most libraries have these books or you may purchase them.

Books:
Greene, Bob, Fulford, D.G. *To Our Children's Children.* New York: Doubleday, 1998.

Hart, Cynthia. *The Oral History Workshop.* New York: Workman Publishing Company, 2009.

Hatcher, Patricia Law. *Producing a Quality Family History.* Salt Lake City: Ancestry, Inc. 1996.

Pfeiffer, Laura Szucs. *Hidden Sources Family History in Unlikely Places.* Orem: Ancestry Publishing, 2000.

Sturdevant, Katherine Scott. *Bringing Your Family History to Life Through Social History.* Cincinnati: Betterway Books, 2000. **This book is out of print but can be found through libraries and used book stores.

Lesson 1: What is Genealogy and Why Should I Care?

Goal

Learn what genealogy is and why it is important. Explore some facts about your family. Learn why it is important to engage your children and grandchildren.

Vocabulary

Ancestors: A person from whom one is descended.

Cousin: First cousins are people in your family who share two of the same grandparents.

Descendants: Those living after a person who are in a direct line such as a son or daughter, grandson or granddaughter, etc.

Genealogy: A study of the family. It identifies ancestors and their information.

Family History: The research of past events relating to a family or families, written in a narrative form.

Interpreter: Someone who describes history through various mediums such as programs, costumed characters, or lectures.

Public History: Practicing history beyond a school environment in places such as historical museums or government agencies.

Social History: The study of the everyday lives of ordinary people.

Tradition: The handing down of statements, beliefs, legends, customs, information, etc., from generation to generation, especially by word of mouth or by practice.

Croom, Emily Anne. *The Genealogist's Companion and Sourcebook.* Cincinnati: Betterway Books, 2003. Read Chapter 1, pgs. 1-9

The Source on Ancestry.com's Wiki. Read the following chapters online:
Overview of Family History Research
http://www.ancestry.com/wiki/index.php?title=Overview_of_Family_History_Research

Basic Record-keeping http://www.ancestry.com/wiki/index.php?title=Basic_Record-keeping

Family History in Time and Place
http://www.ancestry.com/wiki/index.php?title=Family_History_in_Time_and_Place

List of Useful Resources for Beginners
http://www.ancestry.com/wiki/index.php?title=List_of_Useful_Resources_for_Beginners

What is a First Cousin, Twice Removed? By Genealogy.com
http://www.genealogy.com/16_cousn.html

Greenwood, Val D. *The Researcher's Guide to American Genealogy.* Baltimore: Genealogical Publishing Company, 2000.
    Read Chapter 1, pages 3-19

Lesson

THE AUTHOR'S TWINS WONDERING WHAT'S DOWN THE ROAD.

Have you ever sat still and looked down the road and wondered where it goes? Do you wonder if your ancestors ever walked the same road? Wonder if they had similar trials and tribulations as you have in your life?

Have you taken the time to write down your stories for your children and grandchildren? Have you gathered your photos and labeled them so your children and grandchildren will know their ancestors?

If not, why?

Conducting genealogical research allows us to ponder these things and compile the information which can then be passed down through the generations.

Genealogy is the study of the family. The information gathered contains names of ancestors and dates and places where major life events occurred. For some researchers, names and dates are sufficient. For other researchers who want to delve deeper, they seek additional details to create a **family history.**

Family history is the research of past events relating to a family or families, written in a narrative form. Combining these two ideas together allows researchers to compile a more complete history of their family moving beyond names and dates to include the stories of their lives.

Social history is the study of the everyday lives of ordinary people. Examining the more "mundane" details of life can add color to your family history narratives. It brings your ancestors to life. Knowing where we came from and the history of our family gives us roots. It helps us understand why we live where we live, eat what we eat, act the way we do, and have the **traditions** we do.

Where can you learn about social history in the time of your ancestors? Through **public history** events! Public history is practicing history in places such as historical museums or government agencies. For example, the National Park Service provides public history programs in the form of Civil War Battles or Civil War Days. Historical societies and libraries may provide public history in the form of an interpreter dressed as a famous person from history who walks, talks, and lives that person during the program.

Attending a public history event may provide background information on an ancestor. While you may never know what their experience was in a particular time period or event such as a war, public history can give you a basic idea of what it *may* have been like for your ancestor.

Ancestors are people from whom one is descended. This means those people who came before us. You and your ancestors have stories that should be told. How they should be told is up to you. Through these lessons you will trace your family and create a pedigree chart. You might make a photo collage or scrapbook. You will write a short stories about your ancestors. Regardless of how you tell the stories of you and your ancestors, they deserve to be told.

As you work your way through your ancestors and their descendants you may find yourself wondering about **cousins**. *John Howard is my first cousin once removed*. What does that really mean? As you work through your research or hear a family member talk about cousins once or twice removed, refer to the article, *What is a First Cousin, Twice Removed?*, by Genealogy.com. This article has a great table that outlines the connections.

What stories have you heard about your family? Do you have a Civil War, World War I or World War II ancestor? Did your family come to North America on the *Mayflower*? Did they immigrate between the years 1880-1930 when the highest numbers of people came to the United States? Or, are your ancestors or immediate family new immigrants?

While genealogy is the study of the bloodline of a family, many families today have the issue of an adopted child(ren) or step-parents. It is perfectly fine to trace those lines. Genealogy is about making connections with family from the past and family in the present.

Making those connections is especially important as you engage the younger generations in genealogy and family history. Inspire the youth to learn about their heritage through storytelling. Kids are more likely to listen if you have the information presented as a story. Showing photos (when available) helps the child connect to the person in the story.

As you work through the lessons in this book, write down all the questions that come to mind regarding research or an ancestor. Genealogy is a process that requires patience and time. Patience because the information may not always be available or give us a precise answer. Time because it takes time to conduct research and often, as time passes, new information comes to light.

Assignment

Part I: Explore the record sources listed on pages 2-3 of Croom's book from your reading assignment. Write down any interesting site you find and what records or pieces of information may be helpful to you as you research.

Write your thoughts on cluster genealogy and why it is important. How do you think cluster genealogy will help move your research forward?

Part II: Write a story you have heard about someone in your family. Below the story, write the questions that pop into your mind and clues you see that might lead you to more information about that person.

For example:
Frankie Winkler fought in World War II. He fought on Omaha Beach on D-Day in 1944. He was shot and died of his wounds a few weeks later. His father was not sure the remains brought back to the U.S. four years after he died were his.

What thoughts come to your mind when you hear that story? A few that came to the author's mind were:
- In which unit did Frankie fight?
- Was he really on Omaha Beach that day?
- Was he injured that day?
- Why did it take four years to bring his remains home?

The author created a list of things she wanted to know about Frankie and his military career.
- Unit in which he served.
- Dates of service.
- Education and home life.
- How was he killed?
- Where was he buried overseas?
- Find out why it took four years to bring his remains home.

Now it's your turn to write a story or two. Work through the process. You may be surprised at the results.

Additional Resources

Kyvig, David E., Marty, Myron A. *Nearby History Exploring the Past Around You.* United Kingdom: Alta Mira Press, 2010.

Sturdevant, Katherine Scott. *Bringing Your Family History to Life through social history.* Cincinnati: Betterway Books, 2000.

Lesson 2: Where Do I Start? What Do I Need?

Goal

Complete a **pedigree chart**, also known as a family tree and a **family group sheet**.

Vocabulary

Family Group Sheet: A collection of names and facts about one family unit.

Maiden Name: The last name a woman is given at birth.

Maternal: Related through the mother's line.

Paternal: Related through the father's line.

Pedigree Chart: A chart outlining the ancestors of an individual.

Items Needed

You will need a pedigree chart and family group sheet. Examine the following sites and choose the forms you like. Each one is a little different.

Ancestry.com
Ancestral Chart
http://c.ancestry.com/pdf/trees/charts/anchart.pdf

Family Group Sheet
http://c.mfcreative.com/pdf/trees/charts/famgrec.pdf

Blood and Frogs
Genealogy Forms
http://www.bloodandfrogs.com/p/forms.html

Family Tree Magazine
Adoptive Family Pedigree Chart
http://www.familytreemagazine.com/upload/images/pdf/adoptiontree.pdf

Family Group Sheet
http://www.familytreemagazine.com/upload/images/pdf/familygroup.pdf

Standard Pedigree Chart
http://www.familytreemagazine.com/upload/images/pdf/ancestor.pdf

Stepfamily Pedigree Chart
http://www.familytreemagazine.com/upload/images/pdf/stepfamily.pdf

Geneosity.com
Family Tree Forms
http://www.geneosity.com/category/genealogy-forms/family-tree-forms

Family Group Sheets
http://www.geneosity.com/family-group-form/

Relationship Chart
http://www.geneosity.com/relationship-chart/

PBS Ancestors
Pedigree Chart
http://www.byub.org/ancestors/charts/pdf/pedigree.pdf

Family Group Sheets pages 1 and 2.
http://www.byub.org/ancestors/charts/pdf/familygroup1.pdf
http://www.byub.org/ancestors/charts/pdf/familygroup2.pdf

Reading Assignment

Read Genealogy.com's First Steps – Family History Begins at Home
http://www.genealogy.com/79_fs-start.html

Greenwood, Val D. *The Researcher's Guide to American Genealogy.* Baltimore: Genealogical Publishing Company, 2000.
    Read Chapter 2, pages 21-45
    Pay special attention to the sections on Spelling, Relationships, and Naming Patterns

Lesson & Assignment

Pedigree Chart

Grab your pedigree chart and a pencil. It is time to build your family tree!

Completing a pedigree chart or family tree is a visual way to see your ancestors and direct lines. It clearly identifies your parents, grandparents, great grandparents, and so forth. It is the first step in genealogy research.

The chart starts with one person and works backwards through that person's parents, grandparents, great-grandparents, and so on. Write down as much information as you know. It is not necessary to have every detail at this point. Number the chart at the top right hand corner of the page with a number 1.

Begin with person number one to the far left of the page. Write your name in this position and list your birth date and place as well. Next, go to person number two which is your father. Enter as much information as possible from his full name to the dates and places of birth, marriage, and death. Move to person number three which is your mother. List her information. Women should always be written with their **maiden name**. Their maiden name is the surname, or last name they were given at birth, prior to marriage.

Continue on to person four, who is your **paternal** grandfather. Person number five is your paternal grandmother. Add the **maternal** grandparents in spaces six and seven always putting the men on the top line of each family and the woman on the bottom line. Add as much information as possible to your pedigree chart.

If you have filled the chart and can continue farther back, simply put a number 2 in the box next to that ancestral line you want to continue where it says "Cont. on chart no." Then print another pedigree chart and number that chart 2 in the top right hand corner. To add additional charts beyond that just continue to number the ancestral lines and new charts in the same fashion. Place your charts in your binder.

Family Group Sheet

After completing the pedigree chart you need to gather the family group sheets you printed. You will need one family group sheet for each family on your pedigree chart so make extra copies.

The **family group sheet** is an important piece in your genealogical research. These sheets are where you list the family unit. One sheet is completed for each family listed on the pedigree chart and all well as all other family groups (aunts, uncles, and cousins). On these sheets, you will record the names of each set of parents, all the children born to that union, and their vital information. It is important to search **collateral** ancestors because their records may yield clues about your main lines or the family as a whole.

To complete a family group sheet, you should list the names of each set of parents in the top portion of the family group sheet where it has space for husband and wife. This portion of the chart applies whether a couple was married or not married. Please keep in mind it is ok to list a step-parent or adoptive parents in these spaces. The point of this assignment is to make a connection and understand how to gather data on the family.

Next, add the vital information for each parent. Include the names of both the husband and wife's parents. Always remember to list women with their maiden names.

Below the husband and wife is a space for children. Add all children born to that union. The children should be listed in birth order.

A family group sheet should be completed for each family on your pedigree chart. If an ancestor was married multiple times and children were born of those unions, a separate sheet should be completed showing that family group. Store these forms in your binder.

Example Pedigree Chart

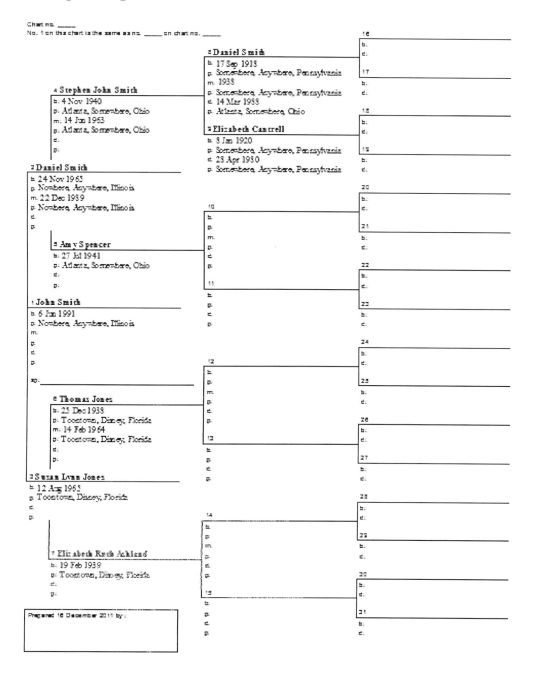

Chart no. _____
No. 1 on this chart is the same as no. _____ on chart no. _____

8 **Daniel Smith**
b. 17 Sep 1915
p. Somewhere, Anywhere, Pennsylvania
m. 1938
p. Somewhere, Anywhere, Pennsylvania
d. 14 Mar 1988
p. Atlanta, Somewhere, Ohio

9 **Elizabeth Cantrell**
b. 8 Jan 1920
p. Somewhere, Anywhere, Pennsylvania
d. 28 Apr 1980
p. Somewhere, Anywhere, Pennsylvania

4 **Stephen John Smith**
b. 4 Nov 1940
p. Atlanta, Somewhere, Ohio
m. 14 Jun 1963
p. Atlanta, Somewhere, Ohio
d.
p.

2 **Daniel Smith**
b. 24 Nov 1965
p. Nowhere, Anywhere, Illinois
m. 22 Dec 1989
p. Nowhere, Anywhere, Illinois
d.
p.

5 **Amy Spencer**
b. 27 Jul 1941
p. Atlanta, Somewhere, Ohio
d.
p.

1 **John Smith**
b. 6 Jun 1991
p. Nowhere, Anywhere, Illinois
m.
p.
d.
p.

sp:

6 **Thomas Jones**
b. 25 Dec 1938
p. Toontown, Disney, Florida
m. 14 Feb 1964
p. Toontown, Disney, Florida
d.
p.

3 **Susan Lynn Jones**
b. 12 Aug 1965
p. Toontown, Disney, Florida
d.
p.

7 **Elizabeth Ruth Ashland**
b. 19 Feb 1939
p. Toontown, Disney, Florida
d.
p.

Prepared 16 December 2011 by :

Example Family Group Sheet

Father	Daniel Smith	
Birth	24 Nov 1965	Nowhere, Anywhere, Illinois
Death		
Burial		
Marriage	22 Dec 1989	Nowhere, Anywhere, Illinois
Father	Stephen John Smith (1940-)	
Mother	Amy Spencer (1941-)	
Other spouse	Susan Lynn Jones (1965-)	
Marriage		

Mother	Susan Lynn Jones	
Birth	12 Aug 1965	Toontown, Disney, Florida
Death		
Burial		
Father	Thomas Jones (1938-)	
Mother	Elizabeth Ruth Ashland (1939-)	

Children

M	John Smith	
	Birth	6 Jun 1991	Nowhere, Anywhere, Illinois
	Death		
	Burial		
	Marriage		

F	Nancy Smith	
	Birth	4 Sep 1968	Toontown, Disney, Florida
	Death		
	Burial		
	Marriage		

Lesson 3: Genealogy Databases

Goal

Learn about the various genealogy databases available for researchers.

Lesson

Genealogists have many options when it comes to recording their family's information. Some prefer to use paper and binders while others prefer to input the data into a genealogy database or an online family tree program.

The different databases and online family trees basically serve the same functions which are to:

- Record the family information and display in tree and family group sheet format
- Allow the input of facts and sources
- To show you potential errors in your data such as dates and names
- Record research plans and questions to be answered
- All the input of media items (photos, video, audio recordings, documents)
- Provide the ability to print reports and charts
- Provide the ability to create family history books
- Share the information with family

While the basic functions are the same, each program has its own pros and cons. It is up to the researcher's tastes and budget as to which program will best suit their needs.

Always check the privacy settings when exploring online family trees. Find out how much information is shared and what you have the power to control. Most online trees allow a private tree option in which you can invite family to view the tree.

A note about Ancestry.com. Ancestry has shaking green leaves next to individual names if there are potential records or a family tree connection for that individual. It is a good idea to view the information and decide on a record by record basis whether or not to include that in your tree. It is not a good idea to accept what someone else has on their tree and merge it into your own. Check the facts first or you may end up with incorrect data and a lot of clean-up work to do later.

Read about the main genealogy databases available. Evaluate each and consider which would be best for your needs.

FamilySearch.org's Personal Ancestor File (PAF) software
https://www.familysearch.org/products
This is a free desktop genealogy program.

Myheritage.com
http://myheritage.com
This site offers a free option to create a family tree which can be shared with others or remain private. For added benefits you have the option to purchase a subscription.

TribalPages.com
http://tribalpages.com/
This site also offers a free option to create a family tree. For added benefits you have the option to purchase a subscription.

WikiTree
http://wikitree.com
This site offers a free family tree with the ability to share publicly or privately with family.

Ancestry.com
http://ancestry.com
This is a subscription-based website that offers a free two-week trial period. You can create family trees on this site and also search for many records. If you only sign up for a free two-week trial be sure to download all the documents you locate and note the source. Most libraries offer a free version of this for in-library use.

Family Tree Maker
http://www.familytreemaker.com/
This is a piece of software created by Ancestry.com to create a genealogy database, track research, attach documents and sources, and run reports.

Legacy Family Tree
http://www.legacyfamilytree.com/
This is a piece of software created to create a genealogy database, track research, attach documents and sources, and run reports.

RootsMagic
http://www.rootsmagic.com/
This is a piece of software created to create a genealogy database, track research, attach documents and sources, and run reports.

Lesson 4: Timelines

Goal

Understand how timelines are helpful in genealogical research. Learn to create a timeline of your life.

Vocabulary

Timeline: The passage of time represented graphically.

Item Needed

Examine the following timelines and print the one you prefer

Geneosity.com's Timeline Sheet
http://www.geneosity.com/genealogy-timeline-chart/

PBS Ancestors Timeline
http://www.byub.org/ancestors/charts/oldpdf/timeline1.pdf

Reading Assignment

Greenwood, Val D. *The Researcher's Guide to American Genealogy.* Baltimore: Genealogical Publishing Company, 2000.
> Read Chapter 3, pages 47-64
> Consider working through a pedigree analysis when creating your timeline and plans to locate information.

"Timelines" from Digital History's website
http://www.digitalhistory.uh.edu/historyonline/timelines.cfm

Using Timelines in Your Research by Donna Pzrecha on Genealogy.com
http://www.genealogy.com/36_donna.html

Lesson

A **timeline** is a drawing that helps us place information in the correct time period. This is typically designed in decade format or year by year depending on how long of a period you wish to capture. Timelines can help us see when big events occurred in the lifetime of an ancestor or family. Not only can we capture big events in an individual's life but also capture local and world history events that were happening during that individual's lifetime.

Timelines in genealogy are very useful for reasons such as:

- Trying to map the migration of a family between certain dates or an entire lifetime
- Understanding where possible records for a family may be kept
- Understanding major life events that happened for a family or individual
- Visualizing an individual's life events to compare to world events.

Examine Ohio State University's ehistory website and the Timelines section. You can search by time period to learn more about world history events that may have affected your ancestors. Categories of timelines include: International Relations and Warfare; Politics; Science, Technology and Discovery; Society and Culture; and Economics and Daily Life. http://ehistory.osu.edu/osu/timeline/timeline.cfm

While you are on the ehistory site, look around. There are many great resources available to researchers.

Assignment

Create a timelines of the following.

- Your life
- The lives of your parents
- The lives of your grandparents
- The lives of your great grandparents

What major events took place that might have affected your ancestors? Create a list on the back of that individual's timeline. Save these timelines and lists because you should refer to them as you progress through the lessons and begin to search for records.

Lesson 5: Sources and Citations

Goal

Understand what a primary and secondary source is, where to find it, and its role in genealogy research. Learn the importance of source citations.

Vocabulary

Citation: Bibliographic origin of evidence.

Original Source: Material that has been unaltered and remains in its original form.

Primary Source: A piece of evidence from the past that was created during the event.

Secondary Source: Sources created after an event by people who do not have firsthand knowledge of the event.

Source: People, documents, artifacts, and print or digital materials.

Special Collection: Collection of rare manuscripts, books, and other materials that is stored in special rooms to preserve the materials in a library or archive.

Item Needed

Finding Primary Sources
http://www.loc.gov/teachers/usingprimarysources/finding.html

Library of Congress: Primary Source Analysis Tool
http://www.loc.gov/teachers/usingprimarysources/resources/Primary_Source_Analysis_Tool.pdf

Analyzing a Document Form
http://www.chicagohistoryfair.org/images/stories/pdfs/2_document.pdf

Analyzing a Photograph Form
http://www.chicagohistoryfair.org/images/stories/pdfs/2_photographs.pdf

Analyzing a Secondary Source Form
http://www.chicagohistoryfair.org/images/stories/pdfs/2_analyzingsecondarysources.pdf

Research Tip 12: Evaluating Written and Oral Evidence on Genealogy.com
http://www.genealogy.com/tip12.html

Greenwood, Val D. *The Researcher's Guide to American Genealogy.* Baltimore: Genealogical Publishing Company, 2000.
      Read Chapter 4, pages 65-78

Mills, Elizabeth Shown. *Evidence Explained Citing History Sources from Artifacts to Cyberspace.* Baltimore: Genealogical Publishing Company, 2009.
      Read Chapter 2, pages 41-90
      Use this as a reference from this point forward in your research.

Lesson

As you gather information in the form of photographs, documents, oral histories, home and hidden sources, it is important to help them understand the differences among source types. Primary sources, secondary sources, and evidence may be difficult concepts for beginning genealogists but should be discussed. Keep in mind that not everything you see or hear is the truth. Evaluate everything before accepting it as fact.

Primary sources are an asset to genealogists. A primary source is a piece of evidence from the past that was created during the event. They provide rich, though not always complete or correct, data. Humans make mistakes and even primary sources will contain spelling errors, incorrect dates, and information omissions.

Examples of primary sources:

- Diaries
- Letters
- Vital records
- Arts-related materials such as photographs, music and design
- Newspaper articles
- Court records and legal documents
- Licenses
- Financial statements
- Probate records such as wills
- Contracts
- Organizational files

A birth certificate is an example of a primary source. A record created at the time of the event. It may, however, contain secondary source material.

Primary sources can help history come alive and should be "listened to" during the research process. Be wary, though, because not everything you read is the truth. Sometimes the truth is stretched to make an event more exciting. Various pieces of evidence should be consulted while examining a topic before drawing conclusions and writing your own piece based on the evidence.

An example of stretching the truth could be when a story is told of a Civil War ancestor who fought at Gettysburg. Maybe the story began as the truth of how the soldier experienced it but over time grew and became a tall tale of how this one soldier saved his entire unit by himself. As with all stories or documents, there is likely some truth to them but it is your job to determine which pieces of information are truth and which pieces are elaborations.

A client recently gave me a copy of a story one of his cousin's had written about their immigrant ancestor. The client wrote notes in the margins concerning facts he thought were incorrect. As I research his family I can use the story and notes to look for clues and records but I keep in mind that 100 people can experience an event and there can be 100 different accounts afterward.

Secondary sources are those created after an event by people who do not have firsthand knowledge of the event. An example of a secondary source is a newspaper or magazine article written after the event occurred, documentary, or book written by people who studied primary sources.

Another example of secondary sources is a birth or marriage date listed on death certificates. The informant was likely not present at either event and therefore could not be the primary source for that information.

Secondary sources can lead researchers to new primary sources. They can also help researchers form an opinion of an event or person. These sources can help answer questions about a topic which will help a researcher narrow their focus or expand a story.

Example

Item: Death certificate completed by the daughter of the deceased.

Facts: Birth date, place, and parent names.

View the death certificate for John Zajicek.
http://www.kidsgenealogy.generationsofstories.net/wp-content/uploads/2012/02/Jan-Zajicek-dc.jpg

Source: Springfield, Illinois, Death Certificates, John Zajicek; death certificate no. 24121, Springfield, Illinois.

The daughter was not present at the birth of her parent therefore this is a secondary source of information. She may know based on hearing this date was the parent's birth and those were the names of his parents, but she was not present at the event.

Citations

An important note about citations. Do not let citations scare you away from doing genealogy research. There are no citation police! In *Evidence Explained Citing History Sources from Artifacts to Cyberspace*, Elizabeth Shown Mills makes a comment about citations being an art form. Everyone starts out in the same place, not knowing the standard way to write a citation. Use the book to help you create your citations. In the end, as long as others can use your citation to locate that piece of information, you are doing it correctly.

A tip – mark the pages with citation types you use most often such as vital records or newspaper articles with a post-it note for faster reference.

Source Citations are important when researching your family's history. When you locate records and add pieces of information into your genealogy you should note the source from which it came. Writing a source citation for the record or book from which you obtained the information allows you and others to recheck the source in the future. It also adds validity to your work.

Source citations in genealogy should go beyond the basic facts of locating the source. They should also identify the type of source (website, book, document, etc.) so accurate analysis can be made.

Assignment

Part I: Locate primary and secondary sources. Compile a list of places near where you live where these sources can be found. Sources can be found in your home; Historical Society; Libraries - research, university, online, and local; Archives - regional and national; Internet; and special collections at libraries and archives. List names and addresses of those near you where you may locate records.

What is a **special collection**? It is a collection of rare manuscripts, books and other materials that are stored in special rooms to preserve the materials in a library or archive. These materials do not circulate. This means they remain on-site and users have to ask permission to view and use the materials.

Part II: Analyze the documents using the National Archives *Written Document Analysis Worksheet* *http://www.archives.gov/education/lessons/worksheets/written_document_analysis_worksheet.pdf*

Next, extract primary information from your documents and add that information to your pedigree chart and family group sheets.

Part III: Cite your sources. Use the reading assignment to help you cite your sources on the documents you have located to this point in your research. Write your source citations on each document.

Additional Resources

Library of Congress Teacher's Guide Resources
- Analyzing Primary Sources
http://www.loc.gov/teachers/usingprimarysources/resources/Analyzing_Primary_Sources.pdf

- Analyzing Books and Other Printed Sources
http://www.loc.gov/teachers/usingprimarysources/resources/Analyzing_Books_and_Other_Printed_Texts.pdf

- Analyzing Manuscripts
http://www.loc.gov/teachers/usingprimarysources/resources/Analyzing_Manuscripts.pdf

- Analyzing Oral Histories
http://www.loc.gov/teachers/usingprimarysources/resources/Analyzing_Oral_Histories.pdf

- Copyright and Primary Sources
http://www.loc.gov/teachers/usingprimarysources/copyright.html

National Archives pamphlet *Citing Records in the National Archives of the United States*
http://www.archives.gov/publications/general-info-leaflets/17-citing-records.pdf

Lesson 6: Direct and Indirect Evidence

Goal

Understand the difference between direct and indirect evidence.

Vocabulary

Direct Evidence: Information relevant to genealogy research that seems to answer a specific question.

Evidence: Something that pertains to an issue in question.

Fact: Something that actually exists; truth; reality.

Indirect Evidence: Information relevant to genealogy research that cannot answer a specific question without other evidence or records.

Proof: Evidence or argument establishing or helping to establish a fact or truth of a statement.

Reading Assignment

Greenwood, Val D. *The Researcher's Guide to American Genealogy*. Baltimore: Genealogical Publishing Company, 2000.
>   Read chapter 4, pages 65-78.

Lesson

When you begin researching your genealogy you start by listing the **facts** you know. Sallie Smith is working on her genealogy she has the following facts: Grandpa Joe Smith was born July 8, 1902 in Chicago, Illinois. He married Wilma Davidson in 1923 in Chicago, Illinois. They had your father Joseph Smith in 1925.

Now, you need to prove this fact and find **evidence** that supports these facts. **Direct evidence** is information that answers a question pertaining to your research. Joe Smith was born in 1902. Direct evidence of this fact may be his birth certificate. The birth certificate lists the date he was born. **Indirect evidence** supporting the fact Joe Smith was born in 1902 may be a 1910 or 1920 census that provides his year of birth. The census may say 1902 but does not provide a full date.

Combining the evidence together makes proof. You can say with greater certainty that Joe Smith was born in 1902 because you have a birth certificate (evidence) and census record (evidence) to support this fact.

Lesson 7: Interviewing Family

Goal

Create a list of questions and learn interviewing skills.

Reading Assignment

Biography Assistant on Genealogy.com's website. Browse the person categories provided.
http://www.genealogy.com/bio/index.html

Research Tip 9: People as Sources for Family History by Raymond S. Wright III, Ph.D., AG
http://www.genealogy.com/tip9.html

Research Tip 10: Preparing to Interview a Witness by Raymond S. Wright III, Ph.D., AG
http://www.genealogy.com/tip10.html

Fifty Questions for Family History Interviews by Kimberly Powell at About.com
http://genealogy.about.com/cs/oralhistory/a/interview.htm

Lesson

Interviewing relatives is a necessary part of genealogy research. It is vital you talk to family members still living and who are able to share information. Ask all the questions you can and gather as many stories, documents and photos as possible during the interviews. Too often we think, "I'll get to that tomorrow" and tomorrow comes and goes and we do not follow through. Then the day comes when the person we wanted to talk to has passed away. Gone are the stories and memories. Or, you wake up and realize you have become the oldest generation and time is passing much more quickly. You feel that need to record the stories and information.

Consider not only talking to the older generation of your family but the younger generation also. Each generation has their own story and gathering these together paints a more vivid picture of the entire family.

Not sure where to begin with interviewing? Don't worry because there are several options. For some, interviewing comes easy, while for others it is more difficult. Read the articles in this lesson and consider the ways you can interview relatives. These could include:

- Write a letter or email to send to relatives which includes interview questions.
- Interview someone in person or over the telephone.
- Video tape or record the interview if the speaker does not mind.
- Transcribe the interview after the video or tape recording.

Areas of interest to consider when developing your interview questions:

- Early life
- Education
- Marriage (consider expectations of the role of each spouse, timing, family life)
- Hobbies and activities
- Sports
- Jobs
- Health issues
- Family traditions (include wedding and funeral traditions)
- Vacations
- Migration or moving from one house or town to another

Assignment

Part I: Before the interviews

- Make a list of people to interview.
- Create a list of at least 30 interview questions. Use the Biography suggestions from Genealogy.com or the article *Fifty Questions for Family History Interviews,* as a guide to add additional questions or discussion topics.
- Interview the relatives on your list.

Part II: After the interviews

- If you took notes, write a story for every interview.
- If you recorded the interview, transcribe it completely.
- Make a list of questions you have after reviewing your notes or transcribing the recording.
- Make a plan to talk to the individual who provided the interview for which you still have questions.
- Make a plan to talk to additional relatives that might shed light on information obtained during the interviews.
- Send thank you notes after the interview so your relatives know you appreciate the time they took to help you.

Part III: Analyze the information
Think about what you learned through the interviews. What new information can you add to your pedigree charts, family group sheets or database?

To prepare for future research after the initial interviews are complete, take a trip to your local library.

The local library is a great resource for genealogical researchers. Many times the library offers databases for research that you can access for free. Some libraries have genealogical collections. Some may also host genealogical society meetings.

Visit your local library. Locate the following:

- Names of interview books such as those listed in the additional resources section.

- List of genealogy database available such as Ancestry.com, Fold3.com, Newspaper Archive, Archives.com, Heritage Quest, and others. Can you access any of these databases at home?

- Does the library have a specific genealogy section? If so, what types of materials does it contain?

- Does the library carry genealogical magazines and journals? Which ones?

- Does the library offer microfilm for genealogy? If not, do they have a microfilm reader? Some libraries do not carry genealogy microfilm but have readers. You can inter-library loan some microfilm.

- Does the library have a genealogy group or host a local genealogical society meeting?

Take notes about your library visit. Include the date of your visit, name and address of the library and names of any librarians you speak with about the collection.

Additional Resources

Greene, Bob, Fulford, D.G. *To Our Children's Children*. Doubleday, 1998.

Hart, Cynthia. *The Oral History Workshop.* New York: Workman Publishing Company, 2009.

Lesson 8: Write a Story

Goal

Complete a brief story about your family based on information collected.

Vocabulary

Biography: A story written about someone.

Reading Assignment

Review the Biography Assistant from Genealogy.com http://www.genealogy.com/bio/index.html

Read *The Secret to Writing a Compelling Family History* http://www.genealogy.com/74_sharon.html

Assignment

Gather together all the charts, interviews, and notes you have at this point. Choose two family groups and write a story about each group. Each story should include: a title, date, author's name, and information collected to date.

Now, choose one ancestor and write his or her **biography**. A biography is a story about someone. Write about all the facts you know. There is no required length for this story.

Your end goal is to have the beginning of a family history book. These three stories can be modified and added to at a later time.

Consider typing these stories into your genealogy database in the notes section for the individual to which they pertain. Later, if you run a report or share the information, the story is included.

Lesson 9: Research Plans and Logs

Goal

Understand the benefits of a research plan, log, and research notes. Create each of these for your genealogical research.

Vocabulary

Research Log: A worksheet that tracks the genealogical sources you have checked, where you found them, what your comments are about the source, and information you discovered.

Research Notes: Notes created during the research process in the form of written comments using photocopies, abstracts, extracts, transcriptions, and translations.

Research Plan: A plan you create to help you (possibly) solve a genealogical problem. Strategically outlines what you know, what you want to know, where you might be able to find it, and how you will go about implementing this plan.

Reading Assignment

Greenwood, Val D. *The Researcher's Guide to American Genealogy.* Baltimore: Genealogical Publishing Company, 2000.
      Read chapter 7, pages 109-124

How to Develop a Genealogy Research Plan from About.com
http://genealogy.about.com/od/basics/a/research_plan.htm

Research Question File
http://www.byub.org/ancestors/charts/pdf/researchquestions.pdf

Lesson

Research plans are a must for every researcher. A research plan outlines what we plan to accomplish while we attempt to find answers to a research question. There are many benefits to creating a research plan.

- Research plans help keep us on track so we do not waste time.
- Research plans help us know what issues we have had and how we attacked them.
- Research plans serve as a refresher when we leave a problem for a while and then return to it.

After your research is complete, write up a research summary. Record your thoughts about the information you located and did not locate. For example, maybe one item on your plan to search was the 1920 Census for a family. You did not find them even after a page by page search. This needs to be noted in your research summary so you do not repeat the same research again if nothing was located.

Research logs are forms that help us plan our research trip and help us keep track of sources we viewed. Logs can be used in a couple of ways. First, take blank forms with you to the repository or library. Fill them out as you research. Second, fill in part of a research log with the sources you know you want to view. Take an extra form for additional items you may discover while you are researching.

The basic function of both forms is to help organize you, your research, and your results. It is a good idea to begin using these at the start of your research rather than wait until you have years of work behind you.

Research notes are created during the research process. Progressing through your research plan and log, you will write down items of interest from the books, manuscripts, maps, photographs, and microfilm you examine. These notes will be beneficial when you return home from a research trip and analyze the information. Include your sources with your notes. Citing your sources is important. It is not something only professional genealogists should be doing as part of their research.

Assignment

Part I: Choose a research problem you are having or identify something you want to know about an individual or family. Make sure this is something you could work on right now. Create a research plan to help you work through this problem or locate information.

Part II: Use the research plan you wrote with the research log and try to solve your problem or locate the information you seek. Write a brief report about your process and results.

Part III: Conduct some research and cite your sources using the plan you created.

Part IV: Write a research summary to store in your binder when you are finished researching. Cite the sources you mention in footnotes.

The research plan example provided below will hopefully give you a few ideas on how to write your own. There is no one correct way. You have to write your plan the way it makes sense to you.

RESEARCH PLAN

Goal(s) or Question(s) to Answer:

Facts Known:

Hypothesis:

Possible Sources:

Research Plan:

Use this log to track your research or create your own log. Logs can be easily created in Excel to record information there or to print.

RESEARCH LOG

Ancestor's Name or Repository:

Objective(s):

Date of Search	Location/Call No.	Description of Source	Comments and questions

Lesson 10: Research Agendas for Libraries and Archives

Goal

Create and carry out a research agenda at a library or archives.

Vocabulary

Archives: a facility that holds and preserves records and historical documents.

Research Agenda: a list of resources held by a library or archives that you wish to search or consult during a visit.

Reading Assignment

Croom, Emily Anne. *The Genealogist's Companion and Sourcebook*. Cincinnati: Betterway Books, 2003.
    Read pages 272-278 of Chapter 8, "Libraries"

Greenwood, Val D. *The Researcher's Guide to American Genealogy*. Baltimore: Genealogical Publishing Company, 2000.
    Read Chapter 5, "An Introduction to Research Tools: The Library," pages 79-90

Lesson

Written by Guest Contributor Shelley Bishop

Now that you understand various types of records and have created a research plan, it's time to venture out to the genealogical department of a library or archives in search of some answers. To make the most of your visit, it's important to know a little bit about the repository and have a research agenda to follow.

The first step is to identify where you want to go. Is there a public library near you with a dedicated genealogy section? Does your local genealogy society maintain its own library? Do you live within driving distance of your state archives or historical society? All of these make good research destinations.

Perhaps one day you'll have an opportunity to visit a major genealogical repository, such as the Family History Library (https://www.familysearch.org/locations/saltlakecity-library) in Salt Lake City, Utah, or the Allen County Public Library (http://www.genealogycenter.org) in Ft. Wayne, Indiana. Because of the huge number of resources they contain, having a research agenda is crucial for these facilities.

Making Your Research Agenda

Your research agenda will be based on two elements: your research plan or goals, and the repository's online catalog. Most libraries today have a digitized catalog that you can search online by title, author, or keyword. A keyword search will give the greatest results. Generally, a good keyword search contains a locality plus a record type. For example, if one of your goals is to determine which cemetery your ancestor from Portage County, Ohio, is buried in, you would enter "Portage County Ohio cemeteries" in the search box. If you want to identify family histories that discuss a particular surname, enter the name along with the word "family" or "genealogy" in the search box.

To create a Research Agenda:
- Print a blank research log from Lesson 9, and put the library's name as the title
- List the items from your catalog search that you want to check at the library
- Note the title, author, and call number for books, and numbers for microfilm
- It's best to make a separate log for each surname you're working on, to save time and effort when you return home to file your research

Many libraries allow you to click on the title of the book or microfilm to get more detailed information. If possible, print the entry out on your printer, and then write a note on it to remind yourself what information you're looking for in that source. Keep it short and simple: "Isaac Taylor, died 1859 in Portage Co.—buried where?" These notes will help focus your efforts on specific research goals in even the busiest or largest repositories.

Gather your research agenda, source printouts, and blank paper for notes into a folder or accordion file to take to the library. It's also helpful to include a family group sheet, pedigree chart, or copy of your research plan. Prepare a pencil pouch or small tote with pens, pencils (some archives don't allow pens), paper clips, and dollar bills for copy machines. Last but not least, check the operating days and hours of the repository and pick a date for your visit.

Visiting the Repository

When you arrive at the library or archives, stop by the reference desk and let a librarian know it's your first visit. Most librarians will be happy to give you a quick tour of the department or point you in the direction of the resources you need. They may offer a map or brochure to help you get oriented. As the day goes on, don't hesitate to ask someone if you have more questions. Reference librarians know their materials. As long as you're respectful of their time and express appreciation for their help, librarians can become some of your greatest research allies.

As you work your way through your research agenda, record the result of each search you conduct on the form. If you find something of interest in the source, write the page number and a note about it in the Comments column. If you didn't, put a short explanatory phrase (such as "Isaac Taylor not found") in that column. Indicating that you examined a source but didn't find what you were looking for saves you from wasting time looking there again in the future. It also shows you made a thorough search.

When you find something useful, make a copy of it for your files. Also copy the title page where the title, author, and copyright information are located, as well as any introductory materials, such as a map or a key to abbreviations. Make sure you have all the elements you'll need to create a source citation for the information. Clip the copied pages to the source page you printed out at home, and jot a brief note about what you found on it as well. Now your materials are ready to be analyzed, recorded, and filed at home.

Having a research agenda to follow helps you make the most of your time in a library or archives. In the next chapters, you'll learn some more methods for organizing and analyzing your research.

Assignment

Part I: Choose a nearby archives or library with a genealogical collection to visit. Find its online catalog. Using a blank research log form and the search techniques outlined above, create a research agenda of sources you want to check there for a particular family or place.

Part II: Visit the library or archives. Find the resources on your agenda and examine them. Record your results, whether or not you found the information you were looking for.

Part III: Make photocopies of information you find, as well as introductory material. Be sure you have all the elements you need to write a source citation for your information.

Additional Resources

Directory of State Archives and Records Programs: list of state and territorial archives by the Council of State Archivists
http://www.statearchivists.org/states.htm

Genealogy Research Libraries: tips, databases, and links for larger libraries on *About.com*
http://genealogy.about.com/od/libraries/Genealogy_Research_Libraries.htm

Libraries, Archives, and Museums: comprehensive alphabetical directory on *Cyndi's List*
http://www.cyndislist.com/libraries/

Research Log Forms
Ancestry.com
    Research Calendar
    http://www.ancestry.com/trees/charts/researchcal.aspx

    Research Extract
    http://www.ancestry.com/trees/charts/researchext.aspx

    Source Summary
    http://www.ancestry.com/trees/charts/sourcesum.aspx

Geneosity
    Genealogy Research Resource Record
    http://www.geneosity.com/research-source-record/

    Genealogy Family Research Journal
    http://www.geneosity.com/family-research-journal/

Lesson 11: Home Sources

Goal

Explore your home for sources that will add information to your family history. Begin to write the stories surrounding those home sources.

Vocabulary

Historical Context: For family history, historical context is placing a person into a specific era or time period in order to view their lives and decisions based on the time in which they lived.

Home Source: A home source is any item or document that will provide facts on people in our family.

Interment: The location where a person will be laid to rest or buried.

Obituary: A notice of someone's death that usually contains a little biographical information about them.

Reading Assignment

The Source on Ancestry.com's Wiki. Read *Home Sources*
http://www.ancestry.com/wiki/index.php?title=Home_Sources

Print and review the PBS Ancestors *Family and Home Source Checklist*
http://www.byub.org/ancestors/firstseries/teachersguide/pdf/checklist.pdf

Lesson

Home sources are valuable to a genealogist. A **home source** is any item or document that will provide facts, clues, or stories about the people in your family. The checklist you printed contains many ideas for possible home sources.

When you find these items, document what they are, who they belonged to, the significance behind them and record the stories. Look beyond your home and ask relatives if they would search their homes or allow you to search with them. Take it even further and talk to your children and grandchildren. Think about all the sources and stories that can be told from old letters to current knick-knacks, to the precious blankets of your grandchildren.

Let's look at a few home sources in more detail.

Household Items

Children's Items

AUTHORS TWINS WITH THEIR AUNTIE PATTI BLANKIES

Look through boxes and bins to find childhood toys, blankets, books, and other items that were saved. Did your child save any old pen pal letters? Are there yearbooks, scrapbooks, grade cards, and pieces of art or school work? What is the story behind these items?

Examine the original story and then what came later. For example, these blankies were given to the author's twins by her best friend in 2005. By 2010, the blankie on the right was so loved it was falling apart. No amount of repairs could save it so it had to be washed, mended, and put away so it would last to show his grandchildren. The story of that blankie and how much he loved it is written in his scrapbook so he will always have that. Record these types of stories.

Family Bible
Examine your family's Bible to see if it contains the names and birth dates, marriage dates, and death dates of your ancestors. Note the name of the person who recorded the information in the Bible. Is this Bible something that has been passed down for several generations?

Family Photographs
Old photographs are a great place to start looking for information. Many times the names of the people are written on the back of the photograph or underneath if the photographs are in a scrapbook or album. Do your grandparents, aunts, or uncles have any that they would share?

Current photographs have stories to tell. Look through your home to locate yearbooks, scrapbooks, loose photos, and framed photos. Can you identify each person in those photographs? Grab a photo-safe pencil and begin noting the names and dates on the backs of the photos.

Furniture
Furniture may provide clues for genealogy. Was any of the furniture passed down through the generations made by someone in the family? Did they sign the back or underside of the piece? Is there a date? Are there stories that go with a piece of furniture? Was that piece received as part of a wedding set or other special occasion? Record these stories. Do you build furniture? Do you sign and date it? Are there stories behind those pieces?

Licenses/Membership Cards
Driver's licenses, hunting licenses, business licenses, and organizational membership cards provide clues as to the activities in which your ancestor participated. Depending on the card, you may find dates of validity, birth dates, addresses, and rank in the organization. Each item will provide a clue to

the life of an ancestor and help send you down other research paths. Again, look for not only your ancestors' cards but your own. Take photos of the cards to add to a family history.

Newspapers
Old and current newspaper articles can provide a wealth of information for a family history. Where can you find old newspapers? Check your attic, old books, photo albums, the family Bible, letters, and inside boxes of memorabilia.

What information can be found in an old newspaper?
- The military history of a family member

- An **obituary** that lists the maiden name of a woman or the names of the deceased's siblings and children. An obituary is a notice of a person's death that usually contains a little biographical information about them. It also includes a notice of the funeral services and **interment**. Interment means where a person will be laid to rest or buried.

- Details about an accident in which your ancestor was involved

- Political information which is helpful if your ancestors were involved in politics

- World history information such as major events that occurred during your ancestor's life time. These details help put your ancestor into **historical context**. Historical context, for family history, is placing a person into a specific era or time period, to view their lives and decisions based on the time in which they lived.

School Records
Look for high school yearbooks which may contain activities in which your ancestors participated. Yearbooks are also a good source to use when proving date and place of graduation.

Report cards are also a good source to track the school(s) attended by ancestors. It is also fun to look at their grades and compare them to yours. Did you and your mom or dad have similar grades in math or science? Or are you a better student in those areas? This type of comparison shows strengths and weaknesses we each have.

Try contacting the schools your ancestors' attended. Find out if they have an archive that holds yearbooks, newspapers, and other records. Can that school provide information about the student or at least confirmation of a graduation date?

<u>Military Records</u>

Did anyone in your family serve in the Revolutionary War, Civil War, World War I or II, or other wars? You can search your house for:

- Service records
  These may provide a serial number, birth date and place, next of kin, beneficiary information, home address, employment information, and dates and locations of service.

- Certificates or official enlistment or discharge papers

Certificates may provide information on an award or medal a soldier earned or show the completion of coursework.

Find out if enlistment records exist for your family members, both ancestors and current. Seek discharge papers which will likely provide an overview of dates and locations of service, birth date and place, previous employment information, home address, and possibly any medals earned.

- Pension files
  Pension files may be found when a soldier applies for aid after retirement or due to injury after a war. Many soldiers applied for a pension after the Civil War. Those files contain many reports about injuries or illnesses, next of kin information, some service information, vital records and death notices.

- Draft cards
  Draft registration cards for World War I and World War II have full name, birth date and place, address, next of kin or closest relative, and employment information.

- Medals or patches from uniforms

These items may not provide many clues but the types of medals or patches will give you a direction in which to go seek additional information. If you know a patch was from the 127th Infantry in World War I, you can look for unit history information to see if your ancestor is listed.

What about unidentified medals and patches? Search online for information and photos and talk to local historical societies, military museums and VFW posts. In talking with these groups and museums, you may uncover new details about your ancestor.

Each of these items will help build the military picture of an ancestor through pieces of information. One item will rarely tell the entire story.

Religious Items

Baptismal or Christening Certificates
Certificates issues upon baptism or christening will usually only contain the name of the church, your name, date of christening, possibly date of birth, and sometimes the names of the parents and godparents.

Death Records
Look for mass cards. Some mass cards or funeral cards may contain birth and death dates as well as burial location. Others may only contain the death date. Regardless, it is a good source of information.

Funeral programs tell a story about the service of the deceased. The program may also list pall bearers and other family members. It may also provide proof of date or year of death, burial date and place, and possibly birth information.

Miscellaneous Church Records

Do you have old church newsletters, bulletins, commemorative books, or other items? These may provide addresses, maiden names, children's names, proof of volunteer work, and possibly school information on ancestors.

Vital Records

Baby Books

A baby book is technically not a vital record but it may contain copies of your birth certificate registered by the state or provided at the hospital. Baby books also contain other personal information about you in the form of height, weight, hair and eye color at birth, immunizations, and illnesses. Many times the book contains a record of the people who visited you in the hospital or provided gifts at a baby shower. Examine those names and addresses to see if you can identify other relatives.

Birth, Marriage, and Death Certificates

Birth, marriage, and death certificates are another good source of information. Details on certificates or licenses may include the names of the person's parents, the birth date and place, death date and place, an address, spouse's name, and other information.

Always keep in mind that you may find a birth date listed on a death certificate that does not match the birth date you found in the family Bible or on a birth certificate. In these cases look for other documents that have the person's birth date on it to try to figure out which is the correct date.

Make it Personal

Think about the time period in which your ancestor lived. What world history events took place? Was there a war? Did any of your ancestors serve in that war? Then explore local history events of that same time period. Is there anything that jumps out at you based on the home sources you discovered?

Now look at your family in the present day. Begin to write your stories. What major world events have occurred in your lifetime? How, if at all, did those events affect you? September 11, 2001, is a major world event that affected all Americans in one way or another. That event might be a good place to start when thinking about historical events.

Field Trip Assignment

Part I: Title a page in your notebook, **Home Sources**. Review the home sources listed in this lesson and the reading assignment. Compile a list of additional sources you can think of in addition to those listed.

Part II: Explore your home and make a list of all the home sources you can find that were discussed in this lesson. Also, include other sources of information you found during your search.

Part III: Review the home sources you discovered and add additional information to your pedigree chart and family group sheets.

Plan a visit: Talk to family members about their home sources. Try to plan a visit to explore their homes and discuss the findings together. You may uncover more than just a few records.

Additional Resources

Geneosity.com's Family Research Journal
http://www.geneosity.com/family-research-journal/

Geneosity.com's Research Source Record
http://www.geneosity.com/research-source-record/

PBS Ancestors How to Select a Record to Search
http://www.byub.org/ancestors/charts/pdf/insert.pdf

Lesson 12: Hidden Sources

Goal

Explore the hidden sources in your home. Begin to write the stories behind those sources.

Vocabulary

Artifacts: Memorabilia passed down through the generations.

Burial File: A file created on a military man or woman who dies while in service. This title was given to files created during World War I.

Hidden Source: A source of information you might not automatically think of when you search for family records.

Individual Deceased Personnel Files (IDPF): A file created on a military man or woman who dies while in service. This title was given to files created during World War II to the present day.

Memorabilia: Items collected and kept because of personal or historical significance.

Lesson

Hidden sources are things that are not automatically thought of when one begins genealogy research. The list of hidden sources in this lesson is by no means comprehensive. These are just some ideas to make you think about the items in your home that may contain pieces of genealogical data.

Think about Hidden Sources in the same way you thought about Home Sources. Each will tell part of a story. Record what the item is, who it belonged to, the significance and story behind the item.

Household Items

Artifacts
Artifacts are memorabilia passed down through the generations. Artifacts usually contain a story and some clues about the ancestor who first owned the artifact.

Dictionaries and Other Books
The author discovered family names and dates on the back side of a torn off cover of a Webster's Dictionary from the 1950s. The author's grandmother had recorded the information here. Why it was recorded here is a mystery. Always check the inside of old books before getting rid of them.

Diaries and Journals
Ask your parents and grandparents, aunts, and uncles, if they kept a diary or journal. Diaries and journals may contain brief bits about a person's life. They may also contain a life history for someone such as a midwife who delivered babies. Many midwives kept a log book of all the babies they delivered. Some have been found to also note the weather and special events in the life of the midwife.

Jewelry
What special jewelry has been passed down through the generations? Where did your ancestors get these pieces? Why was it special to them? What is the story behind the piece?

Postcards or Letters
Did your family send and save old postcards and letters? What about letters from the military or a soldier while he was overseas? What clues can those letters provide? It is unlikely they will tell you exactly where the soldier was stationed but you may gain an idea of how life was while he served.

Postcards and letters may not provide many family clues that will help you trace a line backwards, but can help you tell the story of a person, family, military service, vacation or events happening within the family.

Legal Records

Court Records
Court records may contain a great deal of information about an ancestor or virtually nothing depending on the type of record. Some courts keep court case files for a certain number of years and then destroy all pieces except the verdict or judgment. Other courts keep the files indefinitely. Through these records you may discover additional relatives and details about your family there were previously unknown.

WAR DEPARTMENT
COMMANDING GENERAL, ARMY AIR FORCES
WASHINGTON

January 4, 1943

My dear Mrs. Brouk:

It is with deep regret that I have learned of the untimely death of your husband, Captain Robert Ralph Brouk, on December 19, 1942, in an airplane accident at Kissimmee Airport, Kissimmee, Florida.

It has come to my attention that Captain Brouk was not only a highly skilled pilot, but an officer of rare courage and great charm who captured the affectionate respect of all his associates.

Captain Brouk early proved his valor and fine philosophy of life by serving with the magnificent "Flying Tigers" in the Far East before his transfer to the Army Air Forces. Later, as an instructor at the Orlando Air Base in Florida, he performed important work with great efficiency and was in every respect a credit to his command.

I hope the memory of the gallantry and heroism displayed by your husband in serving his Country, and other nations fighting for the same cause, will be a measure of comfort in your grief, and, with the passage of time, will alleviate your great sorrow.

My deepest sympathy to you and to other members of the family.

Very sincerely,

H. H. ARNOLD,
Lieutenant General, U.S. Army,
Commanding General, Army Air Forces.

Mrs. Robert R. Brouk,
1209 E. Kaley Avenue,
Orlando, Florida.

LETTER FROM WAR DEPARTMENT REGARDING ROBERT'S DEATH. COURTESY VIRGINIA S. DAVIS.

Deeds
Deeds track the ownership of land or property as it passes from one person to the next. The county Record of Deeds Office typically holds these records, although the County Clerk has ownership in some counties. Deeds will list the names of the seller and buyer of property and provide witness names and addresses. A legal description of the property will also be included which will help you locate the places where your ancestors owned land. Just because an ancestor owned land did not mean he lived on that land. Sometimes land was purchased as an investment or to use as additional farm land.

Were your ancestors here prior to 1850? Look for federal and state land sale records or homestead records in your family's papers. These might lead to clues about your rural ancestors.

Immigration and Naturalization Records

Immigration records such as a passport issued by the country from with the person came or a ship manifest (passenger list) may provide many clues about an ancestor and their family.

Naturalization records were created after an immigrant came to the United States and decided to stay. The immigrant would first complete a Declaration of Intention to become a citizen after living in the country a few years. Following that document, the individual would file the Petition for Naturalization and Final Oath. Depending on the time period, these records contain a great deal of personal information about the immigrant, their family, and where they lived prior to immigrating to the United States.

Orphan or Adoption Records

Depending on the time period, records for orphans and adoptions were created. These records may be held in the institution where your ancestor lived or with the court system, although you may discover some in your home.

Probate Records

When a person dies, whether they had a will or not, a probate file may have been created through the court system. A probate record may contain the names and addresses of the heirs of the decedent, personal and real property information, a will, and final settlement details of the estate.

Guardianship records may be part of the probate record set. These records tell the story of how orphaned children were taken care of by another family. These may contain inventories of clothing and supplies purchased for the children, amounts paid each month for school or food or other expenses. These records may lead to additional family member names and information also.

Tax Records

Tax records can provide an idea of a family's financial status at the time the record was compiled. These records are especially helpful if your family once owned slaves. Sometimes the names of the slaves were listed in the records.

Medical Information

Medical Records

Medical records can be difficult to come by because of state and national laws regarding privacy. You may find some in your house. Look in baby books or immunization books that were kept for you or your parents.

Check death certificates for the official cause of death. Ask your family members about family illnesses. Did a certain disease run in your family? Was there a time when many people in the family died due to an epidemic? Record all of this information.

Midwife Records

Was your ancestor a midwife? Many midwives kept a log book of the babies they delivered, fees they charged and collected, and when the birth was registered with the county. Even if your ancestor was not a midwife, if those records can be found in the county in which your ancestor lived it may provide additional proof as to the birth date of your ancestor.

If your ancestor was a doctor, he may have kept records on his patients or a log book of expenses or other office records. Check your home and local historical societies or library collections for these types of materials.

Military Records

Body Transit Records
Did your family have someone who served in World War I, World War II, or beyond, and died during his service? Military men and women who died while in service to their country, abroad or state-side, have a file called a **Burial File** (World War I) or an **IDPF** (World War II and beyond.) Burial Files and IDPFs are files contain service information, serial number, next of kin information, interment and disinterment records, cause of death, and sometimes letters from the next of kin to the government.

Military Memorabilia
The author's grandfather joined the U.S. Naval Armed Guard during World War II. She has in her possession a Bluejacket's Manual dated 1940. This book is falling apart but contains all the information a sailor needed to know in 1940 and through World War II. This book contains the name of the author's grandfather along with his company, his dates of service, and the locations at which he trained. These types of details are excellent to add to your ancestor's military history.

Miscellaneous Information

Archival Collections
This hidden source will likely not be found in your home but in libraries, county and state archives, or university special collections. Look for collections of records based on your ethnicity, location in which your ancestors lived, or the ancestors themselves. You may discover biographies, association records, vital records, photographs, and more.

Biographies and Autobiographies
Look for written accounts of an ancestor's life. These could be something they wrote, or someone wrote about them. As you encounter old family journals and diaries, see what stories you can pull from them to create a biography on an ancestor.

Directories
Books containing addresses before phones were available were called City Directories. These books can help you link family members together and may provide occupational information. After phones were available, City Directories became phone books.

Explore Rural Directories that list farmers, breeders, tractor and silo owners. These directories can paint a vivid picture of the life your farming ancestor led.

Was your ancestor a postmaster? Are there any appointment documents found in your home? Any clues to this occupation? Are there any old postal directories in your home? The National Archives and Family History Library hold appointment registers from 1789 to 1971 on microfilm. Investigate this resource if you have a postmaster in your family.

Genealogies

Has someone in your family completed some genealogical research? Who has those records if they are not in your home? Compiled genealogies are great to examine but always check the facts. Do not take everything as truth as you read through the compilations.

Maps

Look for Sanborn Fire Insurance Maps for the locations in which your ancestors lived. These maps may show, over time, how a piece of property and building(s) changed. Many major cities have Sanborn Fire Insurance Map collections held at libraries and archives. Also look at university libraries in the areas in which your ancestors lived for additional maps. This is especially important if you want to recreate a neighborhood in which your ancestor lived.

Women's Collections

Search for women's history collections through the local library or archives in the area in which your ancestor lived. These collections may provide personal papers, family information, or stories on your female ancestors.

Religious Records

Cemetery Records

Cemetery records may be lying around your home stuck in an old book or box. These records may include plot layouts that tell you who was buried in a specific area of the cemetery. These records help identify family members.

Tombstone and Monument Inscriptions

Look for photographs of your ancestors' tombstones or monuments. What information is contained on the stone? Are there records for these items providing the date of purchase or other information?

Make it Personal

Explore the history behind the artifacts you locate in your home. Did you find an old trunk? What was it used for and when was it used? Do you have an item that has been passed down through the generations? Is it something that relates to world or local events of the time period in which it originated in your family? Are there newer artifacts that are important to you? Write the stories of those and take photographs to include.

Think about the diaries, journals, and letters you may have discovered. Read them and research the history of the time period in which they were written. Does the author discuss local or world events? How do they see things as compared to how you view them?

Field Trip Assignment

Complete the following assignment in your home and local repositories.

Part I: Title a page in your notebook, **Hidden Sources**. Make a list of all the hidden sources you can find in your home. Then visit local repositories, historical museums, and libraries to seek additional hidden sources.

Part II: Review the hidden sources and add information to your pedigree chart and family group sheets.

Additional Resources

Hidden Sources Family History in Unlikely Places by Laura Szucs Pfeiffer.

Lesson 13: Vital Records

Goal

Understand the importance of vital records in genealogical research. Locate and use vital records.

Vocabulary

Birth Certificate: An official document issued when a person is born.

Death Certificate: An official document issued when a person dies.

Marriage License: An official document issued to a couple so they may be married.

Obituary: A notice placed in the newspaper about the death of an individual. Obituaries may include names of other family members, location of burial, employment and service organization memberships, and wake and funeral information.

Vital Records: Governmental records on life events such as birth certificates, marriage licenses, and death certificates.

Reading Assignment

Croom, Emily Anne. *The Genealogist's Companion and Sourcebook.* Cincinnati: Betterway Books, 2003.
> Read Chapter 3, pages 85-97.

Greenwood, Val D. *The Researcher's Guide to American Genealogy.* Baltimore: Genealogical Publishing Company, 2000.
> Read Chapter12, pages 203-232

Red Book: American State, County, and Town Sources on Ancestry.com Wiki
http://www.ancestry.com/wiki/index.php?title=Red_Book:_American_State,_County,_and_Town_Sources   Use this book as a reference guide to help you locate vital records for each state.

Read the entire series of *The Source: Vital Records* on Ancestry.com Wiki
http://www.ancestry.com/wiki/index.php?title=Overview_of_Vital_Records

Vital records are governmental records on life events such as birth certificates, marriage licenses, and death certificates. These records help us establish proof of relationships between people in our family. These records contain both primary and secondary information.

As with other records, the information on vital records may not always be accurate. Some vital records were completed and filed many days or weeks after the birth, marriage, or death occurred. It is possible the midwife or doctor recorded the information incorrectly. Also, keep in mind that there may have been a language issue with immigrants. Typically, a Bohemian woman would have a Bohemian midwife so language should not have been an issue but what was said and what was heard may be an issue. Always check information you find on vital records against other sources.

Early vital records contained less information than vital records of today. Records changed over time and became standardized in the United States. You can view today's standard birth certificate at the links below:

Birth Certificate
http://www.cdc.gov/nchs/data/dvs/birth11-03final-acc.pdf

Death Certificate
http://www.cdc.gov/nchs/data/dvs/death11-03final-acc.pdf

How do these compare to earlier certificates you have located?

A **birth certificate** is the official document that is issued when a person is born. Let's look at an example of two birth certificates and compare the information. The certificates both state they are for Frank Kokoska but the author will show why this is not the case. It is important to reinforce the concept with children that not everything you see and hear is correct.

These certificates belong to the author's ancestors. Frank Kokoska, Emilie Kokoska, and Charles Kokoska were siblings. They were born to Joseph and Majdalena, nee Priban, Kokoska. Majdalena was the mother of eleven children.

Example 1: Birth Certificates

Example: Frank Kokoska

Look up Frank's birth certificate on FamilySearch.org.

1. Visit http://familysearch.org and scroll down to click "United States" under location.
2. Click on "Illinois" on the left column and then click "Illinois, Cook County Birth Certificates, 1878-1922."
3. Search for "Frank Kokoska" and click the certificate for the Frank born in 1882.
4. View the details and then click "View image" on the left side of the screen.
5. You should be looking at this **source:** Chicago, Illinois, Birth Certificate, certificate no. 12756, Frank Kokoska, microfilm no. 7/0048/03.

Facts: Frank Kokoska, male, white, second child of this mother, date of birth 20 October 1882 at 412 W. 17th St in Chicago. Parents are Majdalena Kokoska, nee Skryvan. Father Joseph Kokoska, a laborer.

Analysis: Frank was the second child born to Majdalena and Joseph Kokoska. His birth date and place was confirmed through draft registrations and death records. Majdalena's maiden name which the certificate notes as Skryvan is incorrect. Her maiden name was Priban.

Example 2: Marriage license

A **marriage license** is an official document issued to a couple so they may be married. Marriage licenses and certificates can sometimes tell you a lot about a family, depending on when and where they were created. Some certificates will have additional documents attached indicating the names of the bride and groom's parents, the bride and groom's dates and places of birth, names of witnesses, and their ages. This information can sometimes help prove or disprove a marriage license is for your family.

Example: Let's look at a Chicago marriage license from 1907.

Look up Jaroslav Darda's marriage licence on FamilySearch.org.

1. Visit http://familysearch.org and scroll down to click "United States" under location.
2. Click on "Illinois" on the left column and then click "Illinois, Cook County Marriages, 1871-1920."
3. Search for "Jaroslav Darda" and click the certificate for Jaroslav and Marie Kakuska.
4. View the details and then click "View image" on the left side of the screen.
5. You should be looking at this **source:** Chicago, Illinois, Marriage license, certificate no. 455213, Jaroslav Darda, microfilm no. 7/0039/02.

Facts: A marriage license was issued on 20 April 1907 for Jaroslav Darda, age 24, and Miss Marie Kakuska, age 19. The couple was married on 27 April 1907 by a minister of the Bohemian Congregation of Freethinkers.

Analysis: Marie's last name is misspelled. It was actually Kokoska. She is a sister to Frank and Charles. Additionally, verifying these people are the same people in the author's tree would require examining any of the following: birth certificates, census records, family Bible, interviews, and other sources. Knowing the faith or specific church in which they were married allows the author to possibly examine the church records for more details.

Discussion: View your parents' marriage license and, if possible, your grandparents' license if they have it. How are they the same? How are they different? What information do they contain that you can add to your family history notes? Finally, how do they compare to the license from 1907?

Always keep in mind that names are not spelled the same in every document that you will encounter. Watch for name variations and nicknames.

Example 3: Death Certificates

A **death certificate** is an official document issued when a person dies.

Example: Death certificate of Helen Holik in 1912.

Look up Helen Holik's death certificate on FamilySearch.org.

1. Visit http://familysearch.org and scroll down to click "United States" under location.
2. Click on "Illinois" on the left column and then click "Illinois, Cook County Deaths, 1878-1922."
3. Search for "Helen Holik" and click the certificate.
4. View the details and then click "View image" on the left side of the screen.
5. You should be looking at this **source:** Chicago, Illinois, Death Certificate, certificate no. 21452, Helen Holik, Cook County Clerk's Office, Chicago.

Facts: Helen Holik was listed as a female, single, born in Chicago 19 November 1911. She was 8 years and 26 days old. She died on 15 Aug 1912 at 5:30 pm. Her father is listed as Jan Holik from Bohemia. Her mother is listed as Mary Rataj from Bohemia. The death occurred at 3154 So Ridgway Ave. She was buried at Boh Nat on 18 August 1912. Cause of death is listed as pneumonia.

Analysis: First let's assume no birth certificate was located since vital records were not required in Illinois until 1916. Helen's birth and death fell in between census years so we cannot attempt to verify any information with a census record. We can take this information and add it to the family group sheets with each fact cited as to where the information was obtained.

If a birth certificate was located then we can compare the birth date, parents' names and birth places to that of her death certificate. If she had been born and lived through a census year, provided a census record could be located, we could then compare the information against that record.

Discussion: What other facts found on this death certificate are not listed above? How can these facts help you identify other places to look for records? What other specific records could you look for based on the information on this death certificate? Could you find records at the funeral home or cemetery? Can you think of anywhere else to search?

Final Notes on Vital Records

Vital records were not always a requirement in the U.S. Each state began requiring records to be kept at different times. Use *Red Book: American State, County, and Town Sources* on Ancestry.com Wiki as a reference guide to help you locate vital records for each state. http://www.ancestry.com/wiki/index.php?title=Red_Book:_American_State,_County,_and_Town_Sou rces

Be aware that in addition to the variety of dates in which each state enacted a requirement for vital records registration, state and county boundaries have also changed over time. Knowing where your ancestors lived can help you locate where records can be found. By using maps such as the Newberry Library's Atlas of History County Boundaries Map you can explore boundary shifts from the beginning of the state formation to the present day. As county boundaries changed, the location of records changed.

http://publications.newberry.org/ahcbp/

Another consideration when locating vital records is the possibility of destruction by fire, flood, or war. Many courthouses have had fires that wiped out all records, many of which may not be found anywhere else. When you come across a county like this, look for other record sources that may help you verify the information that you already have or that could help you locate new information.

Assignment

Part I: Locate vital records in your home if you have not already done so. Examine the facts and add the information with source citations to your family group sheets and genealogy database.

Make a list of dates and places that do not match what you previously recorded. You will want to check these facts against other sources.

Part II: Use the Atlas of Historical County Boundaries to identify where the vital records for the ancestors in your main lines may be stored.

Make a list like this:
    Ancestor Name
    Birth: City, county, state where record may exist
    Marriage: City, county, state where record may exist
    Death: City, county, state where record may exist

Part III: Use Ancestry.com's *Redbook* to help identify when those locations began requiring vital records be kept. Add that information to your list.

Part IV: Visit FamilySearch.org's website to see if there are vital records for your ancestors online. http://familysearch.org Save a copy of the records you locate. Then, print copies of those records. Write the source citation on the front of the copy.

If you cannot locate the records online (not all records have been digitized) order vital records through the county clerk or the state's Department of Public Health. Some state archives also hold early vital records.

When you receive the records, examine them and add the information to your family group sheets with citations.

Part V: Locate your state archives website. Search the holdings to see if vital records are held in their collections. Sometimes you can get records at a lower cost through state archives.

For example, the Illinois State Archives holds death certificates from 1916-1947. If you go there in person you can make copies for 50 cents a page. If you order death certificates through the state or county, you could be paying upwards of $10 or $15 per certificate. Can't visit your state archives? See if there is a volunteer in that area who would be willing to do the look-up for you if you pay copy fees and postage. Or hire a professional researcher who does look-ups for set fees.

Part VI: Create a list of vital records you would like to have that were not found on FamilySearch.org. Use *Redbook* or search online for the specific state's vital records office, and record those office addresses.

Order vital records. Some websites allow online ordering while others require you to print a form, complete it and mail it to the office. Follow the steps on each website to order vital records for your family members. *Note: It may take several weeks to receive vital records through the mail.

Part VI: If possible, search the newspapers where your ancestors lived for obituaries. Check with your local library to see if they have any of these papers available online or microfilm. Attempt to locate at least five obituaries. Write a report about your search process and findings.

Some libraries subscribe to NewspaperArchive or GenealogyBank's newspapers. Others may be held in ProQuest. Ask your librarian about these options.

Part VIII: File each copy of a vital record you find in your binder behind the family group sheet to which it pertains. Add the information to your family group sheets and database.

Lesson 14: Census Records

Goal

Understand the value of census records for research between 1790 and 1940. Learn where to find census records and how to search them for ancestors. Complete census transcriptions for each ancestor in your main line. *Note: The 1890 Census was mostly lost due to fire.

Vocabulary

Census: An official count of a population which records specific details about individuals and families.

Enumeration: A numbered list of data.

Enumeration District: A geographic region defined as a tract, area, or district, in which a census is taken.

Reading Assignment

Overview of the U.S. Census Ancestry.com Wiki *The Source*
http://www.ancestry.com/wiki/index.php?title=Overview_of_the_U.S._Census then continue by reading these chapters listed on the right side of the page:
>   *Finding and Reading U.S. Census Records*
>   Each Census year chapter beginning with 1790 – 1940
>   *State and Local Censuses*
>   *Census Substitutes*

Croom, Emily Anne. *The Genealogist's Companion and Sourcebook*. Cincinnati: Betterway Books, 2003. Read Chapter 2, pages 10-82.

Lesson

The U.S. Census is an incredible tool used by genealogists to help prove relationships, migration patterns, and other facts recorded in their family histories. Historians and other researchers use the census as a way to statistically document immigration, migration, local and state history, ethnicity, economics, and other issues.

What is the **census**? It is a count of all the people living in the United States, town by town. The government uses this information to decide where to build more schools, more roads, and where to provide more money and resources. Genealogists use it to find clues.

Historical Background

The U.S. Census was first taken in 1790 after an Article was added to the U.S. Constitution requiring a count of the nation's individuals every ten years. The first census had only six questions. Enumerators were required to record only the name of the family head. It would not be until 1850 when all individuals in a family would be recorded on a U.S. Census. The first census also required the number of free white males broken into two categories - sixteen years and older, and free white males under sixteen. This helped the government identify potential military-aged men. The number of free white females, other persons, and slaves was recorded without age distinction. In some cases the town or district of residence was also recorded.

Until 1850, the census listed the head of the family and a count of others in the household. In 1850 and future censuses, the names of all individuals were added. By 1880, the street name was added with a house number. These addresses are important to keep track of in your notes. They can help you locate people in other records or help prove the person you found is the one you are trying to identify.

Locating Census Records

Where can you find the census? Online subscription sites like Ancestry.com, Fold3.com, and Archives.com hold census records. There are also free sites like FamilySearch.org and Heritage Quest (usually available through your local library) that offer census records. Ancestry.com can also be found for free use through most local libraries.

Repositories like the National Archives and local research libraries also carry the census on microfilm. Sometimes local genealogy societies will transcribe the records and publish them in books or journals.

Census Searching Strategies

Each census index located online was transcribed by different individuals. No two indexes are exactly alike. You might have difficulty locating an ancestor through one index only to find them in another. In addition, one indexer may read a name one way and another indexer may see it completely different if it was not written neatly on the census sheet.

Try a variety of spellings when looking for ancestors. If you are not exactly sure how a surname was spelled, or perhaps it was spelled differently over time, try a wildcard search. A wildcard search means to use an * after part of the word you are searching. For example, I have a surname Kokoska. In an Ancestry.com search I might have no luck finding that surname in a particular census for the Chicago area. I could type 'Koko*' in the surname box, add a first name and other information and see what the search results provide.

Also try a variety of search criteria. Sometimes the search engine will not be able to find your head of household. Try searching for the wife or a child. Add as much information as possible to your search. This means to add the names of all siblings, location where the family was living, birth year or full date, and immigration date if that is an option. Check the search results. If the results do not yield the information you seek, try removing some of the search criteria. Sometimes less is more in a search. Other times more is what you need.

There are times when our ancestors do not appear on a census when we believe they should. There could be many reasons for this.

- They were serving in the military and were not in the country when the census was taken.
- They lived somewhere other than where we thought they should be living.
- The name was spelled so incorrectly that indexes do not find them in a search.
- The family was migrating from one location to another.

Things to consider

After reading Chapter 2 in *The Genealogist's Companion and Sourcebook*, consider the following:

1. Which censuses list military service? How can this information be used to identify possible conflicts or wars in which that ancestor may have served? If these ancestors were still living in 1890, search the 1890 Veteran's Schedule to see if more detailed military information can be found.

2. Examine the relationship abbreviations on page 47. Which of these abbreviations did you find on your census transcriptions? Did you find any questionable relationships (i.e. someone was listed as a brother when that individual was really a son of the head of the family?)

3. Re-read the marriage section on pages 47-48. Calculate the approximate years in which your ancestors married if you did not already locate those facts. Do the approximate years change with each census or remain consistent?

4. Consider consistencies and inconsistencies in the census records. Did you find that immigration or naturalization years were different in various censuses for an individual? What about birth dates? How do you determine which date is correct? Also consider surname spellings. Did an ancestor appear in the censuses with a different spelling each time? If so, note those details in your family group sheets. Names may have been misspelled for a variety of reasons such as the enumerator could not understand the individual providing information; the individual and/or enumerator could not spell the surname properly; or someone other than a family member was providing the information.

5. Consider what other censuses may be available to search for your ancestors such as a Mortality Schedule, Agricultural Schedule, or Manufacturing Schedule. Make a list to search.

6. Review the case studies provided in the chapter. Do you agree or disagree with the results? What would you have done differently?

Part I: Examine your pedigree chart(s) and identify each census year through 1940, in which your ancestors may be found. Write the results as follows listing the number of the person in your main line, his or her name, and the years in which they lived (birth – death). Then list each census in which they may be found and where you think you may find them based on addresses and other information you have collected. For the 1940 Census, before it is fully indexed, you will need to know where you ancestor lived in 1940 to locate them in the census.

<u>No. 4 Joseph John Holik (1906-1964)</u>
1910 – Cook Co., IL
1920 – Cook Co., IL
1930 – Cook Co., IL
1940 – Cook Co., IL

Part II: Print census forms from Ancestry.com for each census year you will search. You will want to print multiple copies so you can transcribe all available censuses for each ancestor in your main line. You can find the forms here: http://www.ancestry.com/charts/census.aspx

Part III: Search online censuses for these records. Many subscription sites offer a free trial period. Consider signing up for one or more of these so you can search from home. Another option is to visit your local library and use the subscription sites there.

Places to locate online census information:

 FamilySearch http://familysearch.org

See if your community has a Local Family History Centers. Microfilm can be ordered through Salt Lake City and viewed at the Family History Center. Many centers have books and on-site films as well. You can search for a Family History Center through FamilySearch.org.

Ancestry.com http://ancestry.com
Fold3.com   http://fold3.com
Archives.com http://archives.com

Part IV: After locating the census records for each ancestor in your main line, download the image and note the source of the image on a printout of the image or in your notebook referencing the image. Then, transcribe the census record for your family on one of the census forms you printed earlier. Repeat this for each census you find for each one of your main line ancestors.

Write the source on the front of the page (if there is room) or on the back so you can properly cite it in your database and notes.

Part V: Analyze the information and add more details to your family group sheets. As part of this analysis you may discover additional family members of which you were previously unaware.

Lesson 15: Social Media

Goal

Interact with others online to further your family history research.

Vocabulary

Blog: Blend of the terms web and log; a place to record your thoughts in journal or diary-like format online.

Hashtag: A tag or keyword embedded in a post on Twitter.

Items Needed

Blog site from Blogger or Wordpress.com

Lesson

Twitter

Twitter is an online platform where people interact in short updates called tweets. A tweet is a status update written in 140 characters or less. Many people add a **hashtag** to their tweets. On Twitter you follow people, meaning you make friends with them. Twitter is public unless you secure your account so you can follow anyone and anyone can follow you, but it does have the block option available.

Hashtags allow users to follow certain topics like genealogy, family history, quilting, the Olympics, and businesses. Hashtags are always preceeded by the # sign. *#genealogy* is an example.

By making friends on Twitter and interacting, you may find some possible relatives. Twitter is also useful for finding genealogy news, learning about new educational opportunities, publications, and conferences.

It is polite to retweet (RT) people's tweets and acknowledge your followers. Retweeting allows your follows to learn about a resource or hear a piece of news. Follow others with similar interests and start conversations. You will be surprised at the conversations you can have in 140 characters or less. Acknowledge your followers also. Tweeting something like, "Thanks for the #follow @jencoffeelover" is polite. People appreciate knowing you see them following you.

FaceBook

FaceBook is an online platform that allows users to share updates, websites, photos, videos, stories, and more. FaceBook allows users to create groups for specific interests. These groups could be surname, ethnic, or locale specific. Search FaceBook for your surnames, locales or ethnicities and see what group results you get. Join the groups that interest you and you may find possible relatives or further your research.

Blogs

We talked about Hidden Sources in a prior lesson. One of those sources was a journal or diary. Do you have a diary? If not, why not? Diaries can be a rich source of family history information. Don't you wish one of your ancestors had left a diary behind for you to read?

Today, many people use an online diary form called a **blog.** Blogs are an online way to share information about your family history and record information. Blogger and WordPress are the two most common platforms available. Explore these with your parents and discuss which site is a better fit for you.

How are blogs helpful to genealogists?

- You are able to share family history information with current family and others you may connect with.
- Other people will read your blog (unless it is private) and may comment on your research.
- One of those comments may help you overcome a brick wall or proceed down a new research path.

Assignment

Project 1: Explore Twitter.   http://twitter.com

Project 2: Explore FaceBook   http://facebook.com

Project 3: Start a blog

There are two very easy to use, free, and popular platforms: Blogger http://blogger.com and WordPress http://wordpress.com. Explore both options and the themes they offer.

1. Start the blog.
2. Choose a theme.
3. Set the privacy level. Some may choose invitation only which means only the people you allow to see your blog can. Others may let it be open so anyone can see it.
4. Add a blog post about your thoughts on these first fifteen lessons.
5. Continue to blog about your genealogy research.

Visit Geneabloggers.com

http://geneabloggers.com

Geneabloggers is a site dedicated to helping genealogists blog. There are many resources for starting a blog and theme ideas for daily blogging. There are also over 2,000 blogs listed and categorized.

Project 4: Follow other blogs.

Explore the functionality of **Google Reader** and then visit Geneabloggers. Explore the many categories of genealogy blogs. Read some of the blogs you find interesting. Subscribe to them through the RSS feed option on the blog. When you subscribe using Google Reader, all of your blogs will be shown there. http://www.google.com/reader

Lesson 16: Health and the Causes of Death

Examine the health and cause of death of each ancestor in your direct line.

Collateral Lines: A line of descent connecting persons who share a common ancestor. These individuals are related through an aunt, uncle, or cousin.

Death Certificate: An official document issued upon a person's death. Certificates usually include the individual's name, date and place of birth, date and place of death, names of parents, cause of death, and location of burial.

Epidemic: A widespread occurrence of an infectious disease. This usually occurs in a community during a specific time period.

Mayo Clinic *Medical History: Compiling your medical family tree*
http://www.mayoclinic.com/health/medical-history/HQ01707

The U.S. Department of Health & Human Services *Surgeon General's Family Health History*
http://www.hhs.gov/familyhistory/

QUESTION: What caused their death?

Many different things caused the death of our ancestors. Death certificates, Family Bibles, obituaries, medical records, and family stories are all ways to discover the cause of death. Have you ever stopped to consider if the things your family members died of were hereditary? Are certain conditions passed down through the generations?

Was anyone in your family a victim of an epidemic such as the Influenza epidemic of 1918? During these time periods you will find many more death certificates with the same cause of death. Tracing death certificates for a family during an epidemic time period may paint a gloomy picture of that family. In some cases many members of the same family were wiped out.

Diseases like cancer, diabetes, thyroid disease, and heart disease, and conditions like depression, autism, and ADHD can run in families. Rarer diseases like sickle cell anemia and hemophilia may also be found within the same family. Understanding and recording the cause of death for not only your direct line but also your collateral lines will help you have a clearer picture of the diseases that may run in your family.

When you visit the doctor today, a medical history is taken not only for you but also your family. Ask your parents if they have completed a medical history at their doctor's office recently. How often do they have to update this information? Is it updated only once a year or at each visit?

Most doctors have questions that include a long list of diseases, such as those listed above, which you should mark if they have been diagnosed in your family. This includes not only your direct line but also collaterals as well. This medical history helps the doctors treat you for current ailments and also helps you try to prevent, or detect early, future ailments or issues.

For example, if diabetes runs in your family, your doctor may suggest exercise and healthy eating to maintain your weight and blood sugar levels. If thyroid disease runs in your family yearly blood draws to check thyroid levels may be suggested.

Keeping track of a family's health history benefits everyone.

Assignment

Part I: Retrieve the death certificates you have located to date. If you do not have many certificates yet, ask other members of your family about relatives who have died and find out the cause of death. Create a list that contains:

- Name of deceased
- Date of birth
- Date of death
- Cause of death
- Contributory factors or causes.

Do you see any trends? Did one cause of death seem to be prevalent? Did that cause run down a specific line in the family? What about the contributory factors or causes? What trends, if any, did you see there? Make notes about these trends.

Part II: Create a family health history. Visit My Family Health History at https://familyhistory.hhs.gov/fhh-web/home.action and fill in the blanks to create your family health history.

Begin with the *Before You Start* pamphlet:
http://www.hhs.gov/familyhistory/start/startenglish.pdf

Then proceed to the *My Family Health Portrait Tool*
http://www.hhs.gov/familyhistory/portrait/index.html
There are versions in different languages and versions you can print.

Save this history and print a copy for your binder. Consider sharing this health history with your family.

*Note: This tool allows you to merge information from Microsoft Health Vault. Discuss using this free tool with your parents. http://www.microsoft.com/en-us/healthvault/

Additional Resources

Daus, Carol. *Past Imperfect.* Santa Monica: Santa Monica Press, 1999.

Gormley, Myra Vanderpool. *Family Diseases Are You at Risk?* Baltimore: Genealogical Publishing Company, 1989.

Old Medical Terminology
http://www.rootsweb.ancestry.com/~usgwkidz/oldmedterm.htm

Lesson 17: Occupations

Goal

Examine the jobs your ancestors held.

Vocabulary

Occupation: A job.

Reading Assignment

Cyndi's List – Occupations Section is full of resources on the names of occupations past and present.
http://www.cyndislist.com/occupations/general/

Occupation List from Rootsweb http://www.rootsweb.ancestry.com/~usgwkidz/oldjobs.htm

Lesson

Occupations can tell you a lot about a person or family and the life they lived. In some cases, the surname of an individual is that of their occupation. Perhaps your Smith ancestor was a blacksmith. Knowing your ancestor was a blacksmith, rather than a plantation owner, in a town in Virginia in the 1700s, gives you an idea of the class or status of that individual or family.

Occupations have changed a great deal over time either through a name change or the disappearance of one occupation followed by the emergence of another. Placing your ancestor in historical context allows you to more fully understand the job they did or why it was called that name. It may help you locate more information on the job or the area in which your ancestor worked. The occupation may lead you to new information on your ancestor through other records and books.

For older occupation names, the Occupation List on Rootsweb in your reading assignment provides a great list of occupation titles and what they mean. For instance, did you know an Accountant used to be called an Accomptant? How about a bar tender as an Ale Draper? A parish man or what we might call a minister or priest was referred to as an Amen Man.

Assignment

Part I: Examine the census transcriptions you made or copies of census records you obtained online. Make a list of the individuals and their occupations. Note the year of the census where the information appeared.

Examine your list of the various occupations held by your ancestors. Are there any patterns to the jobs? Did a father learn a trade and pass that skill down to his sons? Did someone in the family move from a trade to a professional job? Do you see the names of jobs your parents or grandparents held? What about aunts and uncles? How do the jobs of yesterday compare to the jobs of today?

Part II: Consider writing a blog post about the types of jobs held by your ancestors. Be sure to include their names and years of birth and death when you list them in your post. This places them in the historical context which allows readers to more fully understand the jobs they held.

Part III: Attempt to locate occupational records for your ancestors, if any exist. Create a list of possible repositories where the information may be located. For example, if your ancestor worked for the railroad, check with the specific rail line, major research libraries, and railroad museums to begin your search for records.

Lesson 18: Probate Records

Goal

Learn basic details about probate records and how these records are useful.

Vocabulary

Final Accounting: A set of papers in a probate file that outline the complete payment of bills and receipt of payments for an estate.

Intestate: When someone dies without a will.

Inventory: Detailed list of articles of property and their actual or estimated value.

Letters of Administration: Document issued by the probate court to an individual authorizing them to settle the estate of one who dies intestate.

Letters Testamentary: Document issued to the executor of an estate giving authority to settle the estate of one who died testate.

Probate: Legal process of settling an estate.

Proof of Heirship: Testimony documenting the relationships of heirs listed in a probate file to the deceased.

Receipt: Written acknowledgment of receiving something.

Testate: When someone dies with a will.

Will: Document in which a Testator disburses his estate, both real and personal property.

Reading Assignment

Greenwood, Val D. *The Researcher's Guide to American Genealogy.* Baltimore: Genealogical Publishing Company, 2000.
> Read Chapter15, pages 309-330
> Read Chapter 16, pages 331-352
> Read Chapter 17, pages 353-374

Rose, Christine. *Courthouse Research for Family Historians.* San Jose: CR Publications, 2004.
> Read Chapter 6, pages 83-98
> Read Chapter 7, pages 99-110

Records are continually being created for individuals from the time they are born until the time they die. One set of records that may be created are **probate** records. Included in probate records are **wills** and **Proof of Heirship** testimony.

An Example of the Process
When a person ages they might create a will. A will explains what the person wants to give to his or her spouse, children, relatives, and possibly organizations the individual supported.

> I, John Smith, being of sound mind and body hereby declare this to be my last Will and Testament, thereby revoking any former Wills.
>
> First, To my wife Betsy Smith, I bequeath all of my personal and real property. In the event she predecease me, all of my person and real property will be divided between my three children, Albert Smith, Sarah Smith and Kevin Smith, share and share alike.
>
> Second, I request that the amount of $500 be given as a donation to the St. Mary Church in Riverside, Illinois.
>
> Third, I appoint as my executrix, my wife Betsy Smith. In the event she predecease me, then I appoint my son Albert Smith as executor.

That is a very brief example of a will. They can be very complex listing multiple items to be distributed. But wills contain a lot of clues about the family of the deceased. You may find people named and their relationship to the deceased. From the example above, you know that at the time John wrote his will he was married to Betsy Smith. You also know he lists his children as Albert, Sarah, and Kevin. What the will does not tell you is if they are his natural born children or if they are adopted. The will may also provide an idea, depending on how detailed it is, how wealthy the individual may have been.

During the probate process, the will is entered into the Probate Court and must undergo a process to be approved. Once approved, the heirs must be verified through a process called Proof of Heirship. The Proof of Heirship is testimony given by one or more individuals specifically naming the heirs of the deceased, their age, name of spouse if married, and information about the deceased and his spouse.

Probate records entail more than the documents previously described. Additional pieces may include an **inventory, receipts, newspaper notices**, and **final accountings.** Inventories contain a list of each item of value in the deceased's home or work place if they own a business. Receipts contain information on bills paid. Newspaper notices document that the estate was publicized so all debts could be collected. The final accounting contains a complete list of all moneys collected and disbursed during the probate process for a specific estate. All the pieces of a probate file together really paint the picture of part of the life of an individual.

Consider the following from the reading assignment.

1. Who can appoint an executor to an estate, the court or testator? Why?

2. What is a codicil and what was its purpose?

3. What does guardianship mean in an estate? What did a guardian do when granted that title?

4. What does it mean to take an inventory?

5. What is the purpose of a final settlement or final distribution?

6. What kind of family information can be found in a probate file?

7. If your ancestor died without a will, is it still worth it to look for a probate file?

| Assignment |

Part I: Read the will found on FamilySearch.org located here:
https://familysearch.org/pal:/MM9.3.1/TH-1-18268-24580-19?cc=1909099

This is for John Elzy under the following heading: *West Virginia Will Books, 1756-1971 – Kanawha – Will book, v. 148 1959 image 233 of 294*

Locate the following in the will:
- Name of deceased
- Name(s) of family members listed in his will
- Summary of the items he is leaving and to whom
- Name of the estate's executrix/executor/administrator
- Names of witnesses and their address.

Part II: Read the probate file found on FamilySerach.org located here:
https://familysearch.org/pal:/MM9.3.1/TH-266-12125-61324-6?cc=1435692&wc=5052656

This is for Robert Jackson under the following heading: *Vermont Probate Files, 1791-1919, Chittenden County, J, Jackson, Robert (1897, Box 34 File 5637) starting at image 1.*

Locate the following within the records:
- Name of deceased
- List of items found in the probate file
- List a few items found in the Inventory that would not be listed in an Inventory today
- Describe the real estate to be sold and the cost

Part III: Explore other probate files and wills on FamilySearch.org from the 1700s to the present, if they are listed for the states in which your ancestors lived.

Part IV: Locate and obtain probate files for your ancestors. Create a list of people in your main line by their full names, dates and places of death. Then do a GoogleSearch for the addresses of the courthouses or county archives, where these records may be held.

Request a record search on one or more ancestors and attempt to obtain the files. In some cases, there will not be a file. Some families did not have enough property or money to warrant a probate file. Others had a file created when the second spouse died to then disburse the property to the couple's heirs.

Lesson 19: Land Records and Maps

Goal

Learn how land records and maps can help you bring your family to life and lead you down new research paths.

Vocabulary

Abstract of Title: Condensed history to a piece of land. The abstract is only a summary of a deed.

Affidavit: An oath made before any person who is authorized to record an oath.

Deed: A written legal document that authorizes the transfer of property.

Deed of Release: Document signed when the mortgage or other lien is paid on a piece of property. This deed releases the title to the property owner.

Federal-land State: A group of thirty states where land originally was sold by the federal government.

Grantee: Purchaser of property.

Grantor: Seller of property.

Map: Representation of an area of land or sea showing physical features such as cities, roads, mountains, etc.

Migration: The movement of individuals or families from one locale to another.

Mortgage: A conditional transfer of a legal title to a piece of property as security for a debt.

Quitclaim Deed: A deed by which the person releases all title and claim to a piece of property.

State-land States: A group of twenty states where land originally was sold by the colonial or state government.

Trust Deed: A deed where the title is placed in trust, to many people (trustees) to secure the payment of the mortgage.

Warranty Deed: The grantor warrants the deed is good and should the title become faulty, the grantor can be sued.

Reading Assignment

Atlas of Historical County Boundaries   http://publications.newberry.org/ahcbp/

Croom, Emily Anne. *The Genealogist's Companion and Sourcebook.* Cincinnati: Betterway Books, 2003.
> Read Deed Records, pgs. 101-110.

Greenwood, Val D. *The Researcher's Guide to American Genealogy.* Baltimore: Genealogical Publishing Company, 2000.
> Read Chapter 19, pages 399-416 and 423-432.
> Read Chapter 22, pages 477-488

Rose, Christine. *Courthouse Research for Family Historians.* San Jose: CR Publications, 2004.
> Read Chapter 3, pages 27-46
> Read Chapter 4, pages 47-64

Lesson

Land records can tell us a lot about a family and the life they led. Land records may provide proof of family relationships between parent and child or extended family members. They provide a legal description of the property. These descriptions enable researchers to draw them out on a map or sheet of paper. Those drawings can be incorporated into published family histories or genealogy databases.

Deeds are an important part of genealogical research because they can provide clues to new family members or relationships between people. There are many parts of a deed that aid the research we conduct. Let's examine each of these.

- **Names of the parties:** The names of the grantors (sellers) and grantees (buyers) are listed at the top of a deed. In many cases where a husband and wife are selling or buying a piece of property, that relationship will be noted.

- **Legal description of land:** This is a very important piece of a deed. It specifically outlines the exact location of the piece of property being transferred. This legal description can help you locate that property on a map and possibly obtain additional information from the Recorder of Deeds Office where deeds and other records are held.

- **Signatures or marks:** Did your ancestor know how to sign his name or did he use a mark [X] as his signature? Deeds will show you the answer to this question. Signatures are a good thing to collect so you can compare them against other documents, especially if you are trying to determine if that John Smith is your John Smith.

- **Witnesses:** Witnesses were often family, friends, or neighbors. While the deed will not specify the relationship, knowing who these collateral people were can help you in future research. These clues may help you trace the migration of a family or locate them on a census if you are having difficulty locating your family.

- **Recording:** When and where was the deed recorded? Who notarized it and recorded it? As with witnesses, the names of the notary or Recorder or County Clerk may be family, friends, or neighbors. This is especially true in times when counties and towns were very young and had a low population.

In Greenwood's book *The Researcher's Guide to American Genealogy,* read the partial deeds on pages 412-413. What relationships are identified in each deed? Is locating this much information common in all deeds?

The Researcher's Guide to American Genealogy discusses proving relationships through land descriptions on pages 414-415. When genealogists have what problem, does this approach help?

Land records are usually held by the County Recorder or County Clerk. Many are indexed by the names of grantor and grantee. This means that there is usually a set of indexes or books alphabetically arranged by grantor and another set of indexes or books alphabetically arranged by grantee. While not always perfect, land records indexes are extremely helpful in locating records for your ancestors.

Maps

Locating as many deeds as possible for your family can help paint a clearer picture of the migration patterns of your family. Organizing this information by date will also help you trace the migration or expansion or addition of property. Keep in mind that just because someone owned a piece of land did not always mean they actually lived on it. Some farmers owned several tracts of land in a county and may have used that for livestock or crops.

As we move to maps, we can use many of the legal descriptions from the deeds to locate the property where our ancestors lived or owned land. Maps are useful because they give us a visual idea of where our ancestors lived, where they moved, and provide possible migration trails and patterns.

An important concept to remember when it comes to maps is that since the creation of the United States, county and state boundaries have changed many times. Use the Atlas of Historical County Boundaries   http://publications.newberry.org/ahcbp/ to examine your state and county to see how it has changed since 1790 (the earliest date available) or the creation of your state and county.

Maps can also be used to trace migration from one place to another. You may not always know the exact route taken by an ancestor who migrated from Virginia to Kentucky to Missouri. You can examine a map and plot out where your ancestors lived in each state and connect the dots to have a visual idea of where they lived and how they might have migrated.

Things to consider

1. Use the Atlas of Historical County Boundaries   http://publications.newberry.org/ahcbp/
See if your county was part of other counties before it was officially named the county in which you live. What other counties did it belong to prior to the official formation?

2. What other documents may be found in deed indexes in a Recorder's Office? What information might they contain that could help your genealogical research?

3. What kinds of deed books exist? What information can be found in each?

4. What clues can you find in deeds to help your genealogical research? Can you find any evidence of wives?

5. If you have a difficult case and need to help prove or locate additional family members, what other tricks does *The Researcher's Guide to American Genealogy* suggest for research?

Make it Personal

Write down where you live including any other places you have lived during your lifetime. Now list all the places your parents and grandparents lived. Create a list of questions that help form a plan to find out why each individual lived where they did. Ask why they moved, if they moved, and consider the employment they held while living in those locations. Add major world or local events to this list that may have created a reason for people to move from place to place.

If possible, ask your parents and extended family these questions. How many answers can you get?

Assignment

Part I: Write a report about the questions and answers you received in the Make It Personal section of this lesson. Include in your report the names of the people interviewed, the places they lived and especially any historical events that caused the moves or gave them a reason to remain where they were. These clues may lead you to new records.

Part II: Retrieve your census research. Make a list of each head of the family and the address or location where they lived during each census year. For urban dwellers this will usually provide a street address starting with the 1880 census. Searching city directories may help you locate additional addresses or place an individual in time. Rural dwellers may not have a formal street address but perhaps a township name or simply a county. Be sure to note if they owned or rented and if that was a home or farm.

Part III: Choose one ancestral line to work research. Locate a map for the location in which your ancestors lived. Plot on the map their addresses. This may require you to pull street-level maps if your ancestors lived in a city or town or county-level maps if your ancestors were rural dwellers.

Part IV: Attempt to locate property records for your ancestors that owned their homes or land. Search the courthouses or Recorder of Deeds Offices in the counties in which your ancestors lived for these records. If your ancestor purchased Federal Land, consult the **Bureau of Land Management's** website and search for your ancestors. http://www.glorecords.blm.gov/ You may want to search this website for your surnames and the states in which your relatives lived just in case there is a record of which you were unaware.

Project - HistoryGeo

Investigate a new website called HistoryGeo. The company released this information in early 2012. It is reprinted here with permission.

HistoryGeo.com opens its doors with the immediate inclusion of all the maps in both the *Family Maps* and *Texas Land Survey Maps* series of books. These represent nearly 40,000 maps among twenty-three states, all of which display original land-ownership in the context of modern roads, waterways, and other features.

In addition to Arphax's proprietary map library, over 2,000 historical land-ownership maps from Massachusetts, New York, Pennsylvania, Illinois, Indiana, Michigan, Ohio, Nebraska, and Kansas, have also been added. Plans are to increase the breadth of the HistoryGeo.com library to include all of the U.S. and eventually, the world.

With the HistoryGeo Viewer, users can:
* take Snapshots of locations in maps (similar to "favorites" or bookmarks)
* add Custom Markers to Maps, where you can attach:
    o your uploaded images,
    o links to HistoryGeo Snapshots, or
    o URLs to external web-content (link to web-pages of your choice)
* chart and animate migrations,
* designate their Markers as private, public, or to be shared only with friends
* search both within and outside HistoryGeo.com (GNIS searches included, for instance)

Subscriptions choices include a $44 quarterly account, a $66 semi-annual account, or a heavily-discounted choice of $99 per year (a 43% discount).
People interested in this new service are recommended to do the following: 1) Register at www.historygeo.com and take a test drive with instant access to a number of free maps, and 2) take a look at the growing collection of instructional videos found at www.historygeo.com/videos. Once convinced that this is a service for you, simply click "Subscribe", and choose one of the three low-cost subscription options.

Additional Resources

Hone, Wade E. *Land & Property Research in the United States.* Provo: Ancestry Publishing, 1997.

Kashuba, Melinda. *Walking with Your Ancestors A Genealogist's Guide to Using Maps and Geography.* Cincinnati: Family Tree Books, 2005.

Lesson 20: Military Records

Learn about military resources available to researchers and what those records contain.

Bounty Land (Federal): Land promised by the Continental Congress to those who served in the Revolutionary War.

Bounty Land (State): Land promised by the states to those who served in the Revolutionary War.

Burial File: A file compiled during World War I which documented the deaths and burials of U.S. soldiers who died while in service to their country. These documents sometimes contain letters from the family; disinterment records; service records; detailed cause of death; and health or state of the body information.

Compiled Military Service Records (CMSR): A collection of cards placed in a jacket-envelope for a soldier that outlines his military service prior to and through the Civil War.

Draft Registration Cards: Military registration card documenting the vital information of an individual. Not all who registered for the draft fought and others who registered voluntarily enlisted to serve.

Enlistment Records: A record created on a military service man or woman at the time they joined the military.

Discharge Records: A record created on a military service man or woman at the time they left military service.

Individual Deceased Personnel File (IDPF): A file compiled during World War II and beyond which documented the deaths and burials of U.S. soldiers who died while in service to their country. These documents sometimes contain letters from the family; disinterment records; service records; detailed cause of death; and health or state of the body information. (See Burial File)

Military Records: A set of records compiled by the U.S. government regarding an individual's enlistment, service, and discharge from the armed forces.

Pension File: File containing documents pertaining to a set fee paid to a U.S. armed forces veteran for past service to the government. These records sometimes contain service information; birth, marriage, and death records; family information; and health information.

State Bonus Applications: Application files for payments of a bonus to the soldier or his beneficiary after World War I and World War II. These records are typically held in State Archives.

Greenwood, Val D. *The Researcher's Guide to American Genealogy.* Baltimore: Genealogical Publishing Company, 2000.

> Read Chapter 25, pages 551-584
> Read Chapter 26, pages 585-609

From the National Archives website read the sections, "About Military Service Records"
http://www.archives.gov/veterans/military-service-records/about-service-records.html

and

"What Records are Not Available"
http://www.archives.gov/veterans/military-service-records/frequently-requested-records.html

Read the entire section on Military Records on Ancestry.com's *The Source*
http://www.ancestry.com/wiki/index.php?title=Overview_of_Military_Records

Lesson

Wars have been fought since the beginning of time. Records, however, have not been kept since the beginning of time. Where military records exist, you may find a goldmine of information. Military records can tell us a great deal about our ancestors and their families. But, how do you know if you have a military ancestor? Here are a few ways to determine the possibility.

- Locate your ancestor's age at the time of the war. This usually means between the ages of 17 – 40, depending on the war. However, sometimes soldiers may be younger.
- Examine county histories to see if your ancestor is mentioned.
- Look for siblings of your ancestors. Sometimes the ancestor in our direct line did not fight but a sibling did.
- Search the local newspaper for information on those who enlisted, died, or were discharged and sent home.

Types of records available
- **Enlistment Papers**
  These records may contain vital information on an individual.

- **Bounty Land Records**
  This is land promised to those who fought in the Revolutionary War. These records may contain name, rank, and military service information on a soldier.

- **Service records and Compiled Military Service Records**
  Service records outline the locations where a service man or woman served, honors and medals they received, and any disciplinary action taken against them.

- **Discharge Papers**
  These records may provide vital information about the individual, dates of service, honorable or dishonorable discharge information, next of kin, and previous employment information.

- **Pension File**
  Pension files may contain information on next of kin or the service man or woman's entire immediate family if they are married. Additional records may include medical, vital, letters written by the soldier and his family, enlistment, and discharge records.

- **Burial File or IDPF**
  These files were created upon a soldier's death to record how he or she died and where they were buried. These documents sometimes contain letters from the family; disinterment records; service records; detailed cause of death; and health or state of the body information.

- **State Bonus Application Files**
  These records may contain next of kin information, amount paid to the soldier or beneficiary if he was deceased, addresses, and signatures.

Major Wars in U.S. History

Below are a few of the wars fought by U.S. military men and women. This list is by no means comprehensive. The dates of U.S. involvement and types of records you may find are listed with each war.

Revolutionary War (1775-1783)
- Pension file
- Land Bounty records

In *The Researcher's Guide to American Genealogy,* read the declaration and power of attorney filed for heirs of a veteran at the top of page 561. What relationship information can be found in this passage?

Now read the bounty land application at the bottom of page 561. What information can you find in this passage that would help a genealogical search?

Finally, on page 577, what considerations are outlined when searching for Revolutionary War ancestors?

Have you identified any ancestors from the Revolutionary War? How might these records help your research?

Civil War (1861-1865)
- Enlistment papers
- Compiled military service record
- Discharge papers
- Pension file (Confederate pensions would have been filed through the state for which they served, not the U.S. federal government.)

In *The Researcher's Guide to American Genealogy,* on pages 594-598, read the types of records that may be available in addition to the above for Union Civil War soldiers. Now read pages 599-600 and identify records available for Confederate soldiers. Write a brief report about the types of records and what they contain.

Have you identified any ancestors from the Civil War? How might these records help your research?

World War I (1917-1918)
World War I raged from 1914-1918 but the U.S. did not officially join the fight until 1917.
- Enlistment papers
- Service records
- Discharge papers
- Pension file
- Burial file
- State Bonus Application files

World War II (1941-1945)
World War II raged from 1939 -1945 but the U.S. did not officially join the fight until late 1941 after the Japanese attacked Pearl Harbor.
- Enlistment papers
- Service records
- Discharge papers
- Pension file
- IDPF
- State Bonus Application files

Korean War (1950-1953)
- Enlistment papers
- Service records
- Discharge papers
- Pension file
- IDPF

Vietnam War (1960-1975)
- Enlistment papers
- Service records
- Discharge papers
- Pension file
- IDPF

In *The Researcher's Guide to American Genealogy,* page 606 discusses how to obtain information on soldiers from World War I forward. You can learn more about these records through the National Archives website. http://archives.gov.

Have you identified any ancestors from World War I to the present? How might these records help your research? Keep in mind that Korean War and Vietnam War veterans may have their paperwork. If not, they can request it from the government. The records of soldiers who were discharged prior to 1949 are open and available to view or request through the National Archives.

Part I: Visit Fold3.com http://fold3.com and register for a free 7-day trial so you can access military records.

Sign on and click "Records" and "List All Records." Scroll down to "Civil War Service Records."

Select "Confederate Records." Search for "Shannon, Pleasant."

Pleasant Shannon served as a Private in Co. I, Newton's Regiment (2nd Regiment Arkansas Cavalry) in Arkansas. He may also appear in records as Shannon, P M.

Part II: Read through his Compiled Military Service Records on Fold3.com. What details do you find within that record?

Part III: Next, search under "Civil War Service Records" for "Civil War and Later Veterans Pension Index."

Search for Henry A. Hayes who served in Ohio in the 18th and 185th regiments. Pull up his index cards. Save the cards to your computer.

On another tab in your internet browser, go to the National Archives webpage on Veterans Records: http://www.archives.gov/veterans/military-service-records/pre-ww-1-records.html

Learn how to order a pension file. You do not need to order his file, just review the process.

Lesson 21: Religious and Cemetery Records

Learn the value of church and cemetery records and where to locate them.

Baptismal Records: Written facts and documents about the baptism of an individual.

Cemetery: Land set aside for the burial of deceased persons.

Confirmation Records: Written facts and documents about the confirmation of an individual.

Funeral Records: Records outlining the funeral process for an individual.

Grave: Location in a cemetery where a deceased person is buried.

Tombstone: A stone placed on the grave that provides information about the deceased.

Croom, Emily Anne. *The Genealogist's Companion and Sourcebook.* Cincinnati: Betterway Books, 2003.
> Read Chapter 4, pages 120-140

Greenwood, Val D. *The Researcher's Guide to American Genealogy.* Baltimore: Genealogical Publishing Company, 2000.
> Read Chapter 23, pages 489-529
> Read Chapter 27, pages 611-622

Religious Records

Religious records may hold clues to familial relationships, but where can you find the possible religious affiliations of your ancestors?

- Probate records
- Marriage records
- Family stories
- Family Bible
- Census records or city directories – occupation notes

- Death certificates
- News articles

If you know the religious affiliation of your ancestors, where can you find out where religious records held? Contact the local church or parish where your ancestor attended. Some records will be held at the church or parish office. In some cases, an area's records may be held in an archive. For example, the Chicago area Catholic Church records are held at the Archdiocese Office in Chicago rather than the individual churches.

What types of records may be held by a religious organization?

- **Baptismal Records**
  These records may contain the full name of the individual being baptized, names of the parents and godparents, date of birth, and baptismal date. If the church asked the parents and godparents to attend a class to prepare them for the baptism, there may be additional information on file.

- **Confirmation Records**
  These records may contain the full name of the individual being confirmed and possibly his confirmation name. Names of his parents, sponsor, baptismal date, and other information may be available.

- **Marriage Records**
  Religious organizations may have kept a register of those married in the church and the name of the religious leader who performed the ceremony. There may have also been additional information recorded on a certificate or in a marriage file for the couple. If the organization required the couple to attend a pre-marriage class, additional information may be available.

- **Funeral Records**
  Typically a funeral home will keep copies of funeral records, but the religious organization may have a file of its own. Notes about the funeral service and the religious leader's sermon or speaking notes may be contained in those files.

Cemetery Records

A **cemetery** is where we find our deceased ancestors. Records held by a religious organization or cemetery office can help prove genealogical relationships. In addition to the records shown below, cemeteries may have drawings of the tombstones, death certificates, obituaries, and other papers in the decedent's file. Each cemetery is different so always check to see what they hold.

Cemetery offices typically hold identification cards that list the name of the deceased, address, **grave** location, interment date and number, a book and page perhaps, and possibly the age at death and undertaker or funeral home information.

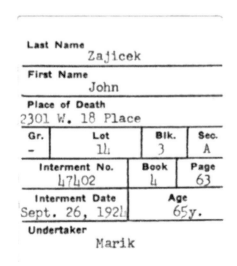

Last Name Zajicek
First Name John
Place of Death 2301 W. 18 Place

Gr.	Lot	Blk.	Sec.
-	14	3	A

Interment No.	Book	Page
47402	4	63

Interment Date	Age
Sept. 26, 1924	65y.

Undertaker Marik

FORM 106 — BP

Source: "Bohemian National Cemetery Grave Index" (card file, n.d., Bohemian National Cemetery), entry for John Zajicek (1924).

In addition to the identification cards, the cemetery holds plot ownership cards and maps which identify who is buried in a plot.

Source: "Bohemian National Cemetery Plot Ownership Cards" (plot ownership files, n.d., Bohemian National Cemetery), plot owned by John Zajicek (1924).

The cemetery plot card to the right lists the interment numbers, names, ages, interment dates, and sometimes the type of container for each person buried in the plot. The card also shows a drawing of the grave locations within the plot.

The people buried in this plot are relatives of the author. Dorothy Zajicek and John Zajicek are the author's great-great-grandparents. They are buried with some of their grandchildren and children.

Notice individual number five, Sylvia Kakuska, after some research, was actually a grandchild with the surname of Kokoska. The same applies with individual number 10, Josef Koska. It should have read Kokoska.

It is important to remember that just as other documents may contain errors, so can cemetery records.

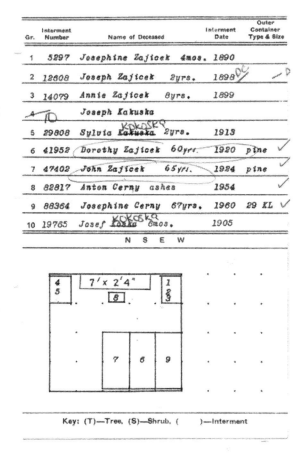

Tombstones may reveal a lot about a person or persons buried in a grave. Names, birth and death dates, relationships, and photographs may provide information we did not have previously.

Source: Jan and Dor Zajicek Grave; grave photograph, privately held by Jennifer Holik [ADDRES FOR PRIVATE USE] Woodridge, Illinois, 2012.

What details about Jan Zajicek's family are provided on this tombstone? Can you find birth and death dates for each individual engraved on the stone? What other details do you notice about the tombstone?

Source: Jan and Dor Zajicek Grave; grave photograph, privately held by Jennifer Holik [ADDRES FOR PRIVATE USE] Woodridge, Illinois, 2012.

Photographs found on tombstones are sometimes the only photographs we can find of our ancestors. Always take several pictures of the tombstone and photographs and details of the stone for your records.

Explore the tombstones of those buried around your relatives. You may discover additional family members nearby that were not buried in the plot for which you were looking.

Assignment

Part I: If possible, explore the records held by a church or other religious organization where your ancestors were involved. What kinds of records did you find?

Part II: Visit a cemetery where your family is buried. Talk to the cemetery office about obtaining records and plot maps. Walk the cemetery and photograph the graves. Write a brief report about your cemetery visit.

Part III: Visit one of these free websites and search for your ancestors. Write a brief report about your findings.

Optional: After your cemetery visit, upload your photos to one of the following websites. Provide as much information as possible with each photograph.

Billion Graves
http://billiongraves.com

Department of Veterans Affairs
http://gravelocator.cem.va.gov/j2ee/servlet/NGL_v1

FindAGrave.com
http://findagrave.com

Interment.net
http://www.interment.net/

Lesson 22: Immigration

Goal

Understand what immigration means and how to locate records for your ancestors.

Vocabulary

Immigrant: An individual who comes from one place to another for the purpose of temporary or permanent residence.

Immigration: To enter a place from another for the purpose of temporary or permanent residence.

Passport Application: An application to travel outside the country.

Port of Entry: The port or city where a ship docked and immigrants entered the United States.

Ship Manifest (Passenger List): A list of passengers on a ship.

Steerage: The lowest part of the ship where tickets were least expensive.

Reading Assignment

Croom, Emily Anne. *The Genealogist's Companion and Sourcebook.* Cincinnati: Betterway Books, 2003.
> Read Immigration and Naturalization pages 387-406

Greenwood, Val D. *The Researcher's Guide to American Genealogy.* Baltimore: Genealogical Publishing Company, 2000.
> Read Chapter 24, pages 531-550

Lesson

The United States has been described as a melting pot because of all the different nationalities that immigrated and make up our nation's people. But where did the **immigrants** come from? How did they get here? What records show their arrival?

Immigration statistics will show that the highest immigration to the United States occurred between the years 1880 and 1930. You can view this and other information on Ellis Island's "The Peopling of America" page here: http://www.ellisisland.org/immexp/wseix_4_3.asp?MID=00122907020054445888& By clicking a time period you can see approximately how many people of each nationality entered the United States.

The reasons our ancestors left their homelands to come to the United States vary. Many of the reasons revolved around hunger, poverty, constant war, discrimination in the form of language, religion, ethnicity, and culture. Many came here for a better life because what they were leaving behind was so horrible.

Our ancestors came in waves, and by that I mean there were times when the Irish were coming to the United States in large numbers. Another way to define "wave" is that the men in the family would come first to start a life and earn money. Later they would send for part or all of the rest of their family, so the family came in waves to the United States. Consider for a moment what it would be like to have your father leave the family to move across the ocean and not return. Perhaps you will wait a year or two (or more!) before you are on a ship crossing that same ocean to meet him. What do you think that would feel like? What do you think it would feel like to leave your grandparents and cousins behind with the possibility that you will never see them again?

Our ancestors boarded ships to bring them from their countries in Europe or elsewhere to the United States. In the 1700s and 1800s, that journey might have taken months. By the late 1800s and early 1900s, the journey may have taken weeks. As ships were better designed and made faster, the journey turned into days.

On the ships, many immigrants traveled in **steerage**. On most ships they were crammed in as tight as they could be packed. The voyage was often rough, and people were sick, yet there was nowhere to go. Once they reached their **port of entry**, relief likely washed over them as the worst of the journey was over. Major ports of entry included Philadelphia, Boston, Galveston, New Orleans, New York, and Baltimore. This list is not comprehensive. There were many smaller ports of entry at which immigrants arrived.

After arriving at the port of entry, the **ship manifest** would be presented and immigrants processed. The most famous port of entry was Ellis Island in New York, which became active in 1892. This large processing station required passengers to be examined to ensure no one entered the country who would become a burden on society, transfer a contagious disease or arrive penniless. Those convicted of a crime were often turned away. Those deemed unfit to enter the country were sent home on the next available steamship.

Many of the ship manifests still exist today and can be found in the National Archives and various places online such as Ancestry.com and Ellis Island.org. Searching these manifests will help you locate information on your immigrant ancestor. Manifests may include, in addition to the name, age, occupation, and country of origin, the following:

- Physical description
- Name and address of nearest family member in the old country
- Name and address of family member they are meeting in the United States
- Amount of money they were carrying.

The information provided depends on the time of immigration. Manifests contained a great deal more information after 1906. Read pages 532-539 in *The Researcher's Guide to American Genealogy* to learn about the main types of passenger lists, where they can be found, and the information they may contain.

Ship manifests may help you uncover additional family members and information about individuals you currently have in your family tree. It is important to note that names were not always spelled correctly. When you search the indexes for your ancestor, look for other spellings. In addition, not all ship manifests survived so there may be times you cannot locate a manifest for a relative.

Things to consider

1. When seeking information on immigrant ancestors, is it a good idea to just "jump across the pond" and start researching or should you start with yourself and work backwards?

2. In what records can you find evidence of immigration? List these records and the information they may contain.

Assignment

Part I: If you have identified immigrant ancestors, create a list. Locate ship manifests for one or more of your ancestors using Ancestry.com or Ellis Island.org.
http://ancestry.com
http://ellisisland.org

Part II: Explore "The Ships List" website. Try to find photographs of the ships on which your ancestors sailed. If you have not identified any at this point, look at some of the ships and their descriptions on the website.
http://www.theshipslist.com/

Note: If you have not yet identified any immigrants in your family, complete the following exercise.

1. Visit Ellis Island.org at http://ellisisland.org

2. Conduct a basic passenger search for the surname **HOLIK**. View the results.

3. Now click "Refine Search" at the top of the page. On this screen in the field for "Name of Town/Village of Origin" type in **SENETIN**. Click search.

4. View the ship manifest for the person that appears.

Lesson 23: Naturalization Records

Goal

Learn the reason for naturalization records and understand the information they may contain.

Vocabulary

Declaration of Intention: A sworn statement, given in court, made by an alien in which he announces his intent to become a citizen of the United States.

Naturalization: A sworn statement, given in court, made by an alien in which he renounces his allegiance to his country of origin and swears allegiance to the United States.

Petition for Naturalization: A document filed after a Declaration of Intention, by the immigrant, declaring their desire to become an official citizen.

Ship Manifest (Passenger List): An official list of all individual's on a given voyage. Information may include name; age; occupation; relative's information; country of origin; town of origin; and physical description.

Reading Assignment

Croom, Emily Anne. *The Genealogist's Companion and Sourcebook*. Cincinnati: Betterway Books, 2003.
> Read Immigration and Naturalization, pages 407-429.

From the National Archives *Prologue* Magazine, read *"Any woman who is now or may hereafter be married . . ." Women and Naturalization, ca. 1802-1940* By Marian L. Smith
http://www.archives.gov/publications/prologue/1998/summer/women-and-naturalization-1.html

National Archives website, "Naturalization Records" section
http://www.archives.gov/research/naturalization/index.html

Lesson

Continuing on an ancestor's journey, after immigration the naturalization process may begin. The reading you did for Lesson 22 also applies to this lesson. If an ancestor did not immigrate, there will be no naturalization papers, unless they married an immigrant at a time when the laws changed. For a period of time between the years 1907 and 1922, if a U.S. born woman married an immigrant (alien), she would lose her citizenship. You will read more about this in the *Prologue* Magazine article in this assignment.

Once an immigrant arrived in the United States, after a period of time, they were allowed to apply for citizenship. The amount of time required for an immigrant to live in the country depended on the time period.

The first step toward **naturalization** was declaring the intention to become a citizen. Immigrants or the courts would complete a **Declaration of Intention** which stated the country from which the immigrant had come and was giving up their allegiance. Early Declaration of Intentions had very little information but as time passed and the 1900s arrived, the forms became more detailed. The information included may be:

- Name of spouse and children
- Specific town of origin
- Date and place of arrival
- Name of ship
- Addresses

The second step toward naturalization was to file a **Petition for Naturalization**. Again, a certain amount of time had to pass before this could be filed. The time was determined by immigration laws. This document also contained the final oath where the immigrant swore allegiance to the United States. Petitions for Naturalizations after 1900 contained a great deal of information about the immigrant and often his family. Depending on the time period, a child who immigrated with his parents was also naturalized when the father swore his oath.

Locating naturalization records can start in one of two places. The first is the county court in the county in which your ancestor lived and was most likely to have been naturalized. The second is the State Archives of the state in which your ancestor was most likely to have been naturalized. The third being the National Archives and Records Administration.

The location may vary from state to state. For example, in Illinois, the U.S. District Court naturalization records are held by the National Archives. County court records (Superior, County, Criminal, and Probate) are held within the counties. The Illinois State Archives itself does not hold naturalization records, but its regional branches known as the Illinois Regional Archives Depository (IRAD), may hold county naturalization records.

Naturalization papers can be found today in the National Archives, local and state archives, and county court archives. In addition to examining the information about your ancestor, pay special attention to the witnesses. Witnesses were often friends, family, or neighbors. Through these collaterals, you may discover additional information on your family. These documents gathered with ship manifests, can provide invaluable evidence about your family.

Things to consider

1. Have you identified anyone on your family tree that immigrated? If so, when did they immigrate? Do you have any of their naturalization documents? Do you know their story?

2. On pages 394-395 of Croom's book it talks about finding evidence of immigration. What kinds of records may hold this information? Do you have any records that provide evidence of immigration?

Part I: After reading the "Naturalization Records" section of the National Archives website, http://www.archives.gov/research/naturalization/index.html
What can you find online through the National Archives website? Where can you find naturalization records pre-1906 and post-1906? Write a brief report about your findings.

Part II: Create a list of ancestors in your tree that immigrated and who may have filed for naturalization.

Make a list of those ancestors, their date of immigration, and where their naturalization records may be held. Attempt to locate and obtain copies of those records.

Example
John Holik   1904   Archives of the Circuit Clerk of the Court, Cook County, IL, or IRAD, or the National Archives

Joseph Kokoska   1880   Archives of the Circuit Clerk of the Court, Cook County, IL or IRAD

Part III: Examine the following sets of naturalization records. Note the following in each set of documents.

- Dates of each set of papers
- Main pieces of information included in each set of papers
- How each set of papers differ
- Explain why the last set of papers may be the most helpful with your research.

Joseph Kokoska
Declaration of Intention
http://www.kidsgenealogy.generationsofstories.net/wp-content/uploads/2012/03/Jos-Koko-Declaration-of-Intent.jpg

Final Oath
http://www.kidsgenealogy.generationsofstories.net/wp-content/uploads/2012/03/Jos-Koko-Final-Nat_-Pg-2.jpg

John Koluvek
Declaration of Intention
http://www.kidsgenealogy.generationsofstories.net/wp-content/uploads/2012/03/John-Koluvek-Declaration-of-Intent.jpg

Petition for Naturalization
http://www.kidsgenealogy.generationsofstories.net/wp-content/uploads/2012/03/John-Koluvek-Naturalization-page-2.jpg

Final Oath

http://www.kidsgenealogy.generationsofstories.net/wp-content/uploads/2012/03/John-Koluvek-Naturalization-pg-1.jpg

And Frank Holik's papers on the following pages.

TRIPLICATE
(To be given to declarant)

No. 109427

UNITED STATES OF AMERICA

DECLARATION OF INTENTION
(Invalid for all purposes seven years after the date hereof)

| UNITED STATES OF AMERICA | | In the | DISTRICT | Court |
| NORTHERN DISTRICT OF ILLINOIS | ss: | of THE UNITED STATES of CHICAGO, ILLINOIS | | |

I, FRANK HOLIK

now residing at 3520 S. 53rd Ct., Cicero, Cook Illinois
occupation Foreman, aged 45 years, do declare on oath that my personal description is:
Sex Male color White, complexion Dark, color of eyes Dark Brown
color of hair Black, height 5 feet 5 inches; weight 196 pounds; visible distinctive marks None
race Bohemian; nationality Czecho-Slovakian
I was born in Senetin, Czecho-Slovakia on November 25, 1890
I am married. The name of my wife or husband is Agnes
we were married on March 13, 1911 at Chicago, Illinois; she or he was
born at Kraselof, Czecho-Slovakia on March 27, 1888 entered the United States
at New York, New York on May 1, 1908 for permanent residence therein, and now
resides at Cicero, Illinois. I have Four children, and the name, date and place of birth,
and place of residence of each of said children are as follows:
Sylvia, born Sept. 16, 1913 in Chicago, resides in Cicero
Frank " Oct. 17, 1915 " " " "
Anna " March 30, 1919 " " " "
Vlasta " August 23, 1923 " Cicero
I have not heretofore made a declaration of intention: Number on
at
my last foreign residence was Senetin, Czecho-Slovakia
I emigrated to the United States of America from Rotterdam, Holland
my lawful entry for permanent residence in the United States was at New York, New York
under the name of Holik, Francisek on March 15, 1910
on the vessel SS Ryndam

I will, before being admitted to citizenship, renounce forever all allegiance and fidelity to any foreign prince, potentate, state, or sovereignty, and particularly, by name, to the prince, potentate, state, or sovereignty of which I may be at the time of admission a citizen or subject; I am not an anarchist; I am not a polygamist nor a believer in the practice of polygamy; and it is my intention in good faith to become a citizen of the United States of America and to reside permanently therein; and I certify that the photograph affixed to the duplicate and triplicate hereof is a likeness of me: So HELP ME GOD.

Frank Holik

Subscribed and sworn to before me in the office of the Clerk of said Court,
at Chicago, Illinois this 25th day of February
anno Domini 19 36 Certification No. 11-126630 from the Commissioner of Immigration and Naturalization showing the lawful entry of the declarant for permanent residence on the date stated above, has been received by me. The photograph affixed to the duplicate and triplicate hereof is a likeness of the declarant.

HENRY W. FREEMAN

[SEAL] Clerk of the U. S. DISTRICT Court.
By Marjorie Theralina Deputy Clerk.

Form 2204-L-A
U. S. DEPARTMENT OF LABOR
IMMIGRATION AND NATURALIZATION SERVICE

Nº 53697

Source: Declaration of Intention, 109427, Holik, Frank, February 25, 1936; U.S. District Court for the Northern District of Illinois; Records of District Courts of the United States, Record Group 21; National Archives and Records Administration– Great Lakes Region (Chicago).

UNITED STATES OF AMERICA
PETITION FOR NATURALIZATION

To the Honorable the ___Bistrict___ Court of ___the United States___ of ___Chicago, Illinois___

The petition of ___FRANK HOLIK___ hereby filed, respectfully shows:

(1) My place of residence is ___3520 S. 53rd Court, Cicero, Ill.___ (2) My occupation is ___Foreman & truck driver___

(3) I was born in ___Senetin, Czechoslovakia___ on ___Nov. 25, 1890___ My race is ___Bohemian___

(4) I declared my intention to become a citizen of the United States on ___February 25, 1936___ in the ___District___ Court of ___the United States___ at ___Chicago, Illinois___

(5) I am ___married.___ The name of my wife is ___Agnes___ we were married on ___March 13, 1911___ at ___Chicago, Illinois___ she was born at ___Kraselof, Czechoslovakia___ on ___March 27, 1888___; entered the United States at ___New York, N. Y.___ on ___May 1, 1908___ for permanent residence therein, and now resides at ___Cicero, Illinois___ I have ___4___ children, and the name, date, and place of birth, and place of residence of each of said children are as follows:

Sylvia, born Sept. 13, 1913, in Chicago, Ill., now resides in Cicero, Illinois
Frank,   "   Oct. 17, 1916,   "   "   "   "   "   "   "   "   "
Anna,   "   Mar. 20, 1919,   "   "   "   "   "   "   "   "   "
Vlasta,   "   Aug. 23, 1923,   "   "   "   "   "   "   "   "   "

(6) My last foreign residence was ___Senetin, Czechoslovakia___ I emigrated to the United States of America from ___Rotterdam, Holland___ My lawful entry for permanent residence in the United States was at ___New York, N. Y.___, under the name of ___Holik, Francisek___ on ___March 15, 1910___, on the vessel ___Ryndam___ as shown by the certificate of my arrival attached hereto.

(7) I am not a disbeliever in or opposed to organized government or a member of or affiliated with any organization or body of persons teaching disbelief in or opposed to organized government. I am not a polygamist nor a believer in the practice of polygamy. I am attached to the principles of the Constitution of the United States and well disposed to the good order and happiness of the United States. It is my intention to become a citizen of the United States and to renounce absolutely and forever all allegiance and fidelity to any foreign prince, potentate, state, or sovereignty, and particularly to ___THE CZECHOSLOVAK REPUBLIC___ of whom (which) at this time I am a subject (or citizen), and it is my intention to reside permanently in the United States. (8) I am able to speak the English language. (9) I have resided continuously in the United States of America for the term of five years at least immediately preceding the date of this petition, to wit, since ___March 15, 1910___ and in the County of ___Cook, Illinois___ this State, continuously next preceding the date of this petition, since ___March, 1910___ being a residence within said county of at least six months next preceding the date of this petition.

(10) I have ___not___ heretofore made petition for Naturalization: Number _____ on _____ at _____ and such petition was denied by that Court for the following reasons and causes, to wit: _____ and the cause of such denial has since been cured or removed.

Attached hereto and made a part of this, my petition for citizenship, are my declaration of intention to become a citizen of the United States, certificate from the Department of Labor of my said arrival, and the affidavits of the two verifying witnesses required by law.

Wherefore, I, your petitioner, pray that I may be admitted a citizen of the United States of America.

I, your aforesaid petitioner being duly sworn, depose and say that I have read this petition and know the contents thereof; that the same is true of my own knowledge except as to matters herein stated to be alleged upon information and belief, and that as to those matters I believe it to be true; and that this petition is signed by me with my full, true name.

___Frank Holik___
(Complete and true signature of petitioner)

AFFIDAVITS OF WITNESSES

___Frank F. Kucera___, occupation ___Trucking business___ residing at ___2805 S. Harding Ave., Chicago, Illinois___ and ___Anton G. Bratyanski___, occupation ___Clerk___ residing at ___3636 S. 53rd Court, Cicero, Illinois___ each being severally, duly, and respectively sworn, deposes and says that he is a citizen of the United States of America; that he has personally known and has been acquainted in the United States with ___FRANK HOLIK___ the petitioner above mentioned, since ___April 28, 1921___ and that to his personal knowledge the petitioner has resided in the United States continuously preceding the date of filing this petition, of which this affidavit is a part, to wit, since the date last mentioned, and at ___Cicero, Illinois___, in the County of ___Cook___ this State, in which the above-entitled petition is made, continuously since ___April 28, 1921___ and that he has personal knowledge that the petitioner is and during all such periods has been a person of good character, attached to the principles of the Constitution of the United States, and well disposed to the good order and happiness of the United States, and that in his opinion the petitioner is in every way qualified to be admitted a citizen of the United States.

___Frank F. Kucera___
(Signature of witness)

___Anton G. Bratyanski___
(Signature of witness)

Subscribed and sworn to before me by the above-named petitioner and witnesses in the office of the Clerk of said Court at ___Chicago, Ill.___ this ___28th___ day of ___April___, Anno Domini 19__38__. I hereby certify that certificate of arrival No. ___11-136650___ from the Department of Labor, showing the lawful entry for permanent residence of the petitioner above named, together with declaration of intention No. ___109427___ of such petitioner, has been by me filed with, attached to, and made a part of this petition on this date.

___HENRY W. FREEMAN___ Clerk

_____ Deputy Clerk

GW

Form 2204—L
U. S. DEPARTMENT OF LABOR
IMMIGRATION AND NATURALIZATION SERVICE

Source: Petition, 198, Holik, Frank, April 28, 1938; U.S. District Court for the Northern District of Illinois; Records of District Courts of the United States, Record Group 21; National Archives and Records Administration– Great Lakes Region (Chicago).

OATH OF ALLEGIANCE

I hereby declare, on oath, that I absolutely and entirely renounce and abjure all allegiance and fidelity to any foreign

The Czechoslovak Republic

prince, potentate, state, or sovereignty, and particularly to...

of whom (which) I have heretofore been a subject (or citizen); that I will support and defend the Constitution and laws of the United States of America against all enemies, foreign and domestic; that I will bear true faith and allegiance to the same; and that I take this obligation freely without any mental reservation or purpose of evasion: SO HELP ME GOD. In acknowledgment whereof I have hereunto affixed my signature.

Frank Holik

(Signature of petitioner)

Sworn to in open court, this 6th day of October A. D. 19 38

...., Clerk.

By.., Deputy Clerk.

NOTE.—In renunciation of title of nobility, add the following to the oath of allegiance before it is signed: "I further renounce the title of (give title or titles) an order of nobility, which I have heretofore held."

Petition granted: Line No. 14 of List No. 3147 and Certificate No. 4508955 issued.

Petition denied: List No. ....

Petition continued from .... to .... Reason ....   14—2818

Source: Petition, 198, Holik, Frank, April 28, 1938; U.S. District Court for the Northern District of Illinois; Records of District Courts of the United States, Record Group 21; National Archives and Records Administration– Great Lakes Region (Chicago).

Lesson 24: Newspapers

Goal

Learn what resources newspapers hold for genealogists.

Vocabulary

Advertisements: Notices which promote a business, service, or product.

Newspaper: Printed publication consisting of folded unstapled sheets. These sheets contain news articles, correspondence, weather, advertisements, obituaries, and travel information.

Obituary: Notice of the death and funeral of an individual in a newspaper.

Social Column: A column that records the comings and goings of people in the town or city, also records births, engagements, marriages, and deaths.

Reading Assignment

Croom, Emily Anne. *The Genealogist's Companion and Sourcebook.* Cincinnati: Betterway Books, 2003.
>   Read Special Collections pages 227-246

Greenwood, Val D. *The Researcher's Guide to American Genealogy.* Baltimore: Genealogical Publishing Company, 2000.
>   Read Chapter 11, pages 183-202

Lesson

A **newspaper** contains a lot of information. That information varies from paper to paper but will always contain the latest news, updates on news from prior days or weeks, weather, **obituaries**, **advertisements**, and sports. Older newspapers may also contain a **social column** of this family visiting someone in town or a couple's engagement or marriage. The social columns may provide religious affiliation clues in addition to the names of the individuals and their activities.

Obituaries vary in their content but contain the name of the deceased and usually names of some of his family members. Military information is often included which provides clues as to where to obtain additional information. Other items may include residential address of the deceased, occupation, name of the funeral home and cemetery, and time of the wake and funeral. Use obituaries as a stepping stone to locate new information on your family.

Newspapers are printed daily in cities across the country. Many are now available online, through sites such as *Newspaper Archive* or *ProQuest*. Many libraries offer newspaper databases as part of their services. You can access some of these from home. Check with your local library as to which they offer.

What about old newspapers that are no longer in print? Many old newspapers are being microfilmed and stored in libraries, archives, and historical societies. Some of those newspapers are also being preserved online through the companies listed above. You can also see if there are printed or online indexes or compilations of articles created by local genealogy societies or historical societies. Locating an ancestor in an index may allow you to order a copy of the obituary or newspaper article through a library or archive.

Using obituaries, news articles, advertisements, and social columns together, you may be able to piece together a picture of your family at a given time in history. Pay special attention to local and world news as you read the newspapers. Placing your family in historical context provides new research avenues. For example, an obituary you read states an ancestor fought in Company L, 127th Infantry, 32nd Division and died in France in 1918. This information tells you the following:

- This ancestor fought in World War I (Look for military records)
- He died in 1918 (Request his Burial File for World War I)
- What is the date of the newspaper in which his obituary appears? Was there a notice of his death after it was reported to his parents? How long after his death were his remains brought home? (Regardless of the date, see if there is another notice either at the time of his death or his burial.)
- Names of his relatives (Locate additional vital records, obituaries, census records)
- Burial location (Request cemetery records, photograph the grave.)

Use these clues to locate new information about your family.

Examine newspapers whenever you search for family. You may be surprised at the amount of information that can be obtained.

Assignment

Visit your local library and see if they have any online newspaper collections. Search these collections, if possible, for your ancestors.

Lesson 25: Ephemera

Goal

Learn what ephemera is and the process to help you discover your family stories.

Vocabulary

Ephemera: Paper items that were originally meant to be only kept for a short while; they are now often sought after by collectors and some can have substantial monetary value.

Identification Clues: In the context of ephemera, this would include names of individuals along with age(s), date(s) and location(s) that have been handwritten or typewritten onto the ephemera piece.

Transcribe: In the context of ephemera, to make a written or typewritten copy of all handwritten and typewritten messages and/or notes found on both the front and back of a piece of ephemera.

Reading Assignment

"Discovering a Wildcatter" by Caroline M. Pointer in the May 2010 online issue of the *Shades of the Departed Magazine*
http://issuu.com/shadesofthedeparted/docs/shadesmayissue?mode=embed&layout=http%3A%2F%2Fs
kin.issuu.com%2Fv%2Fcolor%2Flayout.xml&backgroundColor=FFFFFF&showFlipBtn=true

The 48 Hour Ephemera Challenge Forum
http://48hourephemerachallenge.lefora.com/

"Home Sources" from *The Source* located online on Ancestry.com's Wiki.
http://www.ancestry.com/wiki/index.php?title=Home_Sources

Lesson

1. Identify ephemera that the family possesses. Look for family ephemera that has identification clues on it. At the very least, a name of an individual is needed. However, a name with an age, a location and/or a date is even better. The types of ephemera include:

- Letters
- Envelopes
- Postcards
- Greeting Cards
- Photographs and Photo Albums
- Business Cards
- Calling Cards
- Invitations

- Report Cards
- Rewards of Merit
- Playbills or Programs
- Newspapers or Newspaper Clippings
- Scrapbooks
- Autograph Books
- Books Given as Gifts
- Diaries or Journals

2. If the ephemera piece is found in a collection of other ephemera pieces, then notate that. They could be related and might be helpful in researching. In fact, researching the entire collection may be necessary to find the family story.

3. Ask family members to identify who once owned the ephemera piece or to identify the creator of the ephemera piece. Also ask if they know anything else about the piece. If possible, visit with the creator of the ephemera piece in order to obtain more clues.

4. If the ephemera piece has a handwritten or typewritten message, transcribe the message. For books, do not transcribe the entire book, just the handwritten message as well as any notes found written throughout the book.

5. List all the identifying clues that can be found on the front and the back of the ephemera piece. If there is more than one page, then create lists for each page, front and back. For books, include the publishing information, especially the publication date. The goal of this step is to date the ephemera piece as well as to create a central listing of clues.

6. Research any historical information surrounding the ephemera piece. Include world, country, regional, and local period history.

7. Research both online and offline using the list of clues to look for primary and secondary sources to find direct and indirect evidence. Documents will help to make the connections providing more names, locations, and dates, which in turn will be helpful when you begin to search newspapers, articles, books, etc. for family stories. However, sometimes the family story comes directly from the information contained in the documents, as can be the case with a death certificate.

8. When looking for more than one person who is listed on a piece of ephemera – such as a letter or postcard – it is important to research the family trees of each person in hopes of discovering a connection between the persons mentioned.

Make it Personal

Inventory your home for family ephemera. Also visit with other family members and determine whether they have any family ephemera that once belonged to an ancestor. Discuss the ephemera pieces with family members to obtain clues to the pieces.

Assignment

Complete the following assignment.

Part I. Take one piece or a collection of pieces of family ephemera and apply the above 8-step process.

Part II. Create a family story based on the information, evidence, and documentation found after completing the 8-step process.

Additional Resources

Webfooters Postcard Club
http://www.thewebfooters.com/html/postcard_dating.html

Metropolitan Postcard Club of New York City: Guide to Real Photo Postcards
http://www.metropostcard.com/guiderealphoto.html

Shiloh Postcards: A Brief History of Postcards
http://www.shilohpostcards.com/webdoc2.htm

Cost of US and World Postage Stamps
http://www.costofstamps.net/

Junior Philatelists on the Internet: United States Postage Stamps
http://www.junior-philatelists.com/USStampsHistory.shtml

Tips for Dating Old Photographs
http://www.billblanton.com/date.htm

Hats and Hair: Fashion History of Hairstyles
http://www.fashion-era.com/hats-hair/index.htm

The Costume Detective: How to Date Old Photographs by the Costume
http://www.fashion-era.com/Dating_Costume_History_Pictures/index.htm

Wikipedia
http://www.wikipedia.org/

Google Search
https://www.google.com/

The Red Leather Diary: Reclaiming a Life Through the Pages of a Lost Journal by Lily Koppel

Lesson 26: Examine it Once, Twice, and Again

Understand that documents, research reports, books, and the like must be read more than once to fully grasp every piece of evidence provided. Learn that reviewing these items and your work from time to time may yield new clues and realizations about your family history.

Lesson – A Case Study

This is an example of an issue the author recently had with a marriage license issued to her grandparents. The author has two documents for her grandparents, Joseph Holik and Libbie Brouk. One is a Marriage License issued 19 April 1930 in Chicago. This license states they married on the same day. The certificate portion of the license was signed by a Judge of the Circuit Court of Kewanee, IL named H. Sterling Pomeroy.

The first document: View Joseph Holik and Libbie Brouk's marriage license.
http://www.kidsgenealogy.generationsofstories.net/wp-content/uploads/2012/03/Joseph-Holik-m-Libbie-Brouk-marriage-license.jpg

The second document is a fancy Certificate of Marriage for Joseph Holik and Libbie Brouk. The second document was signed by a Judge of the Circuit Court of Kewanee, IL named H. Sterling Pomeroy.

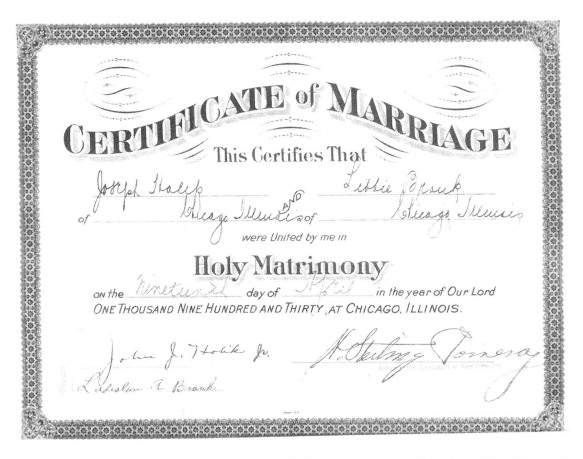

Source: Joseph Holik and Libbie Brouk, 1930; Certificate of Marriage, privately held by Jennifer Holik [ADDRES FOR PRIVATE USE] Woodridge, Illinois, 2012.

Did the couple marry in Kewanee, Illinois? Why, in 1930, would the couple drive from Chicago to Kewanee to get married? The author's friend had a similar marriage license and was asking the same questions. Initial glances at the documents "say" the couple was married in Kewanee but is that correct? No.

Let's break this down and look at the clues.

- The marriage license was issued in Chicago, Cook County, Illinois.
- The certificate portion on the bottom states the couple was indeed married in the County Building in the city of Chicago.
- The address given is 226 County Building, Chicago, IL.
- The Judge signed his name and stamped "Judge of the City Court of Kewanee, IL."

It was discovered after some online research that this Judge spent time serving in the Cook County Courts.

Why would you break down a document more than once? Sometimes you think you pulled all the details out but when you go back to it later, after more research is done, you may see something you "missed" before. It may have been something that didn't mean anything to you at the time. Reviewing documents for an individual after more research is done sometimes sparks a new research idea or shows a clue that now has greater meaning.

Upon first glance at both of these documents you think both couples drove to Kewanee to get married. Breaking down the details you find out that was not the case.

Assignment

Select a family in your tree and review the documents you have collected to this point. Are there any new clues that you see? Is there anything that makes more sense to you after additional research was conducted? Write a one-page report on your findings.

Lesson 27: Travel and your Family History

Goal

Plan a family history research trip that is organized

Vocabulary

Repository: A place or building where things are or may be stored.

Items Needed

Atlas
MapQuest.com   http://mapquest.com

Lesson

Written by Guest Contributor Terri O'Connell

Planning a research trip can be a fun activity for your family. Trips are a good teaching tool when it comes to understanding the areas from which your family came. You will also find that you require the use of mapping and math skills.

To have a well-planned research trip, one must first decide in which area they want to research and second, what records are available in that area. Places you might look for records are: genealogy libraries, cemeteries, archives, churches, and courthouses. Always call ahead before visiting any repository or library to check on hours and inquire about the records you seek. In some cases, materials may need to be pulled prior to your visit.

While compiling this list of potential repositories to visit, it is imperative to keep track of all information for each location. This would include the name of repository, address, phone number, contact name, hours of operation, what their collection holds, security policy, and photocopy fees. Create a spreadsheet that keeps all of this information together. It will make visiting the repositories easier.

Looking beyond repositories and cemeteries, there are other places you might want to consider seeing on a research trip. These include your ancestors' prior work locations, residences, and churches. These places are great photography opportunities for your family. Also, consider bringing a video camera and creating a video of the places that are personal to your family. One of your parents or siblings can video you as you play the reporter on the scene giving the camera all the information about the location and the ancestors who once lived there.

Assignment

Create a research trip.

Part I: Explore the areas in which your ancestors lived. What repositories and libraries are in that area? Create a list that includes the name of the repository and its address.

Part II: Use Mapquest.com to create a map of repositories you would like to visit. Add all of the above locations one at a time to create your map. Next, search for hotels and motels in the area that are in your price range.

Tip
See if the hotels offer free Wi-Fi and breakfast. Wi-Fi will be important if you decide to keep a blog about your trip or if you want to update an online family tree with information you have found.

Part III: After creating a map and locating a place to stay, create a plan detailing how you will divide your time between each repository. Most importantly, remember to leave time to do the actual research. Sometimes, this can be a full-day process.

Project

Use the atlas to figure out your driving directions for your research trip. Based on those directions, see if there are any other points of interest where you could stop along the way.

Tip
If you take this research, trip talk with the locals to learn about the history of the town as well as how it has changed over time.

Lesson 28: Storing and Organizing Paper and Digital Files

Goal

Understand how to handle and care for the material you acquire while researching your family history.

Vocabulary

Clipping: A piece cut from a newspaper or magazine.

Document: A written or printed work that can be used as evidence or proof.

Ephemera: Mementos or souvenirs.

Photograph: An image made using a camera.

Scrapbook: A blank book in which documents, photographs, clippings, and ephemera are combined.

Stable: To keep something safe and secure to prevent it from being damaged or destroyed.

Reading Assignment

Read the American Association for State and Local History Technical Leaflet
http://www.msa.md.gov/msa/refserv/pdf/aaslh.pdf

Lesson – Paper Files

Written by Guest Contributor Laura Cosgrove Lorenzana

Throughout these lessons you've found, received, or acquired many different types of material. Documents, photographs, clippings, and ephemera are all part of a family history collection. Because we work so hard to research and collect these items, they should be organized, cared for, and kept stable so they last a very long time. The first step is to learn the basic ideas for care and handling. The second step is to understand the best place to store the material. The third step is to organize and store these materials.

For the purposes of these lessons, much of what you've gathered and/or created is being stored in a binder. There are different types of plastic, some of which are not intended for long-term storage of paper material. Plastic is often produced with additives that actually cause harm to paper and photographs. Purchase plastic that is either polypropylene or mylar to ensure long-term protection for the material.

Materials you wish to store flat can be stored using acid-free folders and boxes. These storage materials can be purchased from most office supply stores or through archival companies such as Hollinger Metal online. Acid-free containers help keep the paper chemically stable.

Care and Handling
What is the best way to handle the material that you've gathered? Wash your hands with plain soap and warm water before sitting down with your material. This is important because your hands naturally have oils in them. These oils, when transferred to the paper can cause it to deteriorate and/or hold dirt. When handling photographs, make certain to hold them on the edges, or if you can, wear white cotton gloves. You'll often see workers in museums and archives wearing gloves when they're handling material.

When picking up a document, always support it from the back. If you have documents, like old letters, that are folded, it's best to gently unfold them, put them between two pieces of acid-free paper and either put them in a mylar protector or an acid-free folder. The act of folding and unfolding a document breaks down the paper, and, if it's done too much, will eventually tear apart the paper.

Documents should not be stored with paper clips, staples, binder clips, or post-it notes. The metal in the clips can rust or tear the paper. There are chemicals in the adhesive in the post-it notes that is very harmful to paper and can either discolor it or cause it to degrade.

By handling your materials with care and storing them in a comfortable location, they will last for many years.

Storage of Materials
Documents and photographs on paper need to be protected from a variety of things that can harm them. Simple things like temperature, humidity, light, and pests can greatly affect how long paper lasts.

The key to long term storage of family history is A KIC! Always Keep It Comfortable. Materials need to be stored somewhere that *you* would be comfortable. Are you comfortable when it is really hot or really cold or when the temperature varies a lot? What about if it's very humid or very dry?

Remember to give your material AKIC:

The temperature should be between 60-70° Fahrenheit (15-21° Celsius) and the Relative Humidity between 40-50%. Why are temperature and humidity important? If the humidity is too low, the paper can become very dry and brittle causing it to fall apart when it's handled. If the humidity is too high, the material becomes damp which increases the chances for mold to grow. Mold is very bad as it quickly spreads and destroys paper.

There should be plenty of air movement.

Direct sunlight can cause fading, so keeping materials out the sun is also suggested.

Material should be kept in a place where there aren't any creepy, crawlies; no spiders, roaches, centipedes, mice, etc. Why is this important? Well, other than the gross factor, bugs and rodents carry dirt and bacteria on their bodies that when passed onto the paper can cause it to deteriorate. Many pests eat paper or use it to make nests.

Organization of Materials

Every person adjusts how they label and organize their material in their own way; however, these guidelines should assist you in creating a solid foundation on which to build your collection. Organizing your material is important for several reasons. It helps to ensure that you can easily find something when you need it, that you don't have to handle the material you have over and over as you look for something, and that the material you have is safe and stable.

Think of the organization of your paper files the same way you would your digital files. You can use either archival quality polypropylene enclosures in a binder or acid-free folders that can be stored in an archival box. In either case, organizing material by surname generally works best. Folders should be labeled using pencil. Why pencil? Getting in the habit of using pencil when working with your material is best because pens, markers, and other materials like that are permanent. Should they break or spill, they can permanently harm your paper and/or photographs. So, take care and use pencil.

Labels can be as simple as just the surname (i.e., Jones); however, as your collection grows, you may want to separate each person into their own folder/protector. In that case, the label should include the surname, given name, and a range of dates. The range of dates helps to keep individuals with the same name (Jones, John) separate. You can also add other identifying information on the outside of the folder, such as spouse (husband or wife), children, or where the person is buried. The folders can then be stored in alphabetical order by surname, then given name and, if you'd like, by the range of dates.

Lesson – Digital Files

Many of the records we view and use today are initially found online in digital format. We print and save these files throughout the course of our research, but do we have a way to organize and store them so they are easily located later? Digital files require just as much care in organization as your paper files. Here are some suggested steps to organize your digital files.

Step 1
Create a folder in your "My Documents" folder for "Genealogy."

Step 2
Create new folders within the "Genealogy" folder for each surname in your pedigree tree.

Step 3
Move the files you have downloaded into the appropriate surname folder.

Optional
To maintain more order when many records are downloaded and saved to your computer, consider creating folders within each surname for each record type, i.e. census, immigration, naturalization, military, and vital records.

Digital Organizational Resource
Sort Your Story   http://sortyourstory.com

Sort Your Story is a software program that allows you to create family files in which you can organize photos and documents for individuals in your family. This very visual program helps any level of researcher organize their files but it is particularly helpful to children and young adults. Organizing your records and notes in Sort Your Story helps you identify gaps in your research and build a more complete family history.

Assignment

Part I: Organize your paper files using the system outlined in the lesson.

Part II: Organize your digital files using the system outlined in the lesson.

Optional: Locate a suitable space in your home to store your family history collection. Remember to give the material A K I C. Closets are excellent spaces for keeping material stable. Space can often be made on a shelf which is better than the floor. Or, if you have desk space or a desk drawer these would work as well. Don't forget to add your family history collection to your family's emergency plan too!

Additional Resources

Caring for Your Family Archives
The U.S. National Archives website has many resources for preserving family papers and memorabilia.
http://www.archives.gov/preservation/family-archives/

The Northeast Document Conservation Center (NEDCC.)
A nonprofit, regional conservation center specializing in the preservation of paper-based materials. NEDCC serves libraries, archives, museums, historical societies and other collections-holding institutions, as well as private collections.
http://www.nedcc.org/resources/family.php

Sort Your Story Software
Digital organization software that is an excellent way for kids to learn genealogical organization.
http://sortyourstory.com

Lesson 29: Putting it all Together

Goal

Write the beginnings of a family history starting with yourself and an ancestor using the materials you have discovered.

Vocabulary

Autobiography: A story about your life, written by you.

Biography: A story about someone's life written by someone else.

Final Project

Part I: Write a brief autobiography that describes your family and your life.

Include the following:
- Title page and name of author, date of autobiography
- Your full name and birth information
- Names of your parents and siblings
- Information about your parents and siblings
- Information about education, hobbies and activities
- Anything else interesting about you that you want people to know
- Photographs.

The total length of your autobiography should be three to five pages.

Part II: Write the biography of one of your ancestors. Include all the information you have discovered throughout this project for that ancestor and his or her family.

Include the following:
- Title page with the name of the author and date of biography
- Name of the ancestor and siblings and parents
- Vital information on each family member
- The story of the ancestor using the records you located. Cite your sources
- Social and local history to place the ancestor in proper historical context
- Photographs, maps and other items that will enhance the story.

The total length of your biography should be 8-10 pages depending on how much information you have collected about this particular ancestor.

Lesson 30: Where to Go From Here

Online Courses and Articles

Consider expanding your genealogical knowledge online.

Archives.com Expert Series
http://www.archives.com/experts/

Brigham Young University Independent Study
http://is.byu.edu/is/site/courses/free.cfm
BYU offers some free genealogy courses.

FamilySearch offers many courses and videos here:
https://www.familysearch.org/learningcenter/home.html
Also search their Wiki for more specific information on ethnicity, county, state, and country resources. https://www.familysearch.org/learn/wiki/en/Main_Page

Family Tree University
http://www.familytreeuniversity.com/
On occasion FTU offers some free courses.

National Genealogical Society
http://www.ngsgenealogy.org/cs/educational_courses
There are some free courses for NGS members.

National Institute of Genealogical Studies
http://www.genealogicalstudies.com/
On occasion NIGS offers some free courses. Courses range from beginner to intermediate.

Give Back to the Community

Consider becoming an indexing volunteer for FamilySearch.org. Learn more here:
https://www.familysearch.org/volunteer/indexing

Join a genealogy society and become involved in projects or working with other researchers. Many societies offer courses through the society or local library. Some also hold annual conferences. In addition, society meetings provide great educational opportunities because the topics change monthly.

Glossary

Abstract of Title: Condensed history to a piece of land. The abstract is only a summary of a deed.

Affidavit: An oath made before any person who is authorized to record an oath.

Ancestors: A person from whom one is descended.

Artifacts: Memorabilia passed down through the generations.

Autobiography: A story about your life, written by you.

Biography: A story about someone's life written by someone else.

Birth Certificate: An official document issued when a person is born.

Blog: A place online to record thoughts in journal or diary-like format.

Bounty Land (Federal): Land promised by the Continental Congress to those who served in the Revolutionary War.

Bounty Land (State): Land promised by the states to those who served in the Revolutionary War.

Burial File: A file compiled during World War I which documented the deaths and burials of U.S. soldiers who died while in service to their country. These documents sometimes contain letters from the family; disinterment records; service records; detailed cause of death; and health or state of the body information. (See IDPF)

Census: An official count of a population which records specific details about individuals and families.

Citation: Bibliographic origin of evidence.

Clipping: A piece cut from a newspaper or magazine.

Collateral Lines: A line of descent connecting persons who share a common ancestor. These individuals are related through an aunt, uncle, or cousin.

Compiled Military Service Records (CMSR): A collection of cards placed in a jacket-envelope for a soldier that outlines his military service prior to and through the Civil War.

Death Certificate: An official document issued upon a person's death. Certificates usually include the individual's name, date and place of birth, date and place of death, names of parents, cause of death, and location of burial.

Declaration of Intention: A sworn statement, given in court, made by an alien in which he announces his intent to become a citizen of the United States.

Deed: A written legal document that authorizes the transfer of property.

Deed of Release: Document signed when the mortgage or other lien is paid on a piece of property. This deed releases the title to the property owner.

Derivative Source: Material that is manipulated through copying such as extracts, transcriptions, abstracts, translations, and authored works.

Descendants: Those living after a person who are in a direct line such as a son or daughter, grandson or granddaughter, etc.

Direct Evidence: Information relevant to genealogy research that seems to answer a specific question.

Discharge Records: A record created on a military service man or woman at the time they left military service.

Document: A written or printed work that can be used as evidence or proof.

Draft: Selective requirement for service in the U.S. armed forces. This was for naturalized white or native-born citizens, male, age twenty-one and older.

Draft Registration Cards: Military registration card documenting the vital information of an individual. Not all who registered for the draft fought and others who registered voluntarily enlisted to serve.

Enlistment Records: A record created on a military service man or woman at the time they joined the military.

Enumeration: A numbered list of data.

Enumeration District: A geographic region defined as a tract, area, or district, in which a census is taken.

Ephemera: Mementos or souvenirs.

Evidence: Something that pertains to an issue in question.

Fact: Something that actually exists; truth; reality.

Family Group Sheet: A collection of names and facts about one family unit.

Family History: The research of past events relating to a family or families, written in a narrative form.

Federal-Land state: A group of thirty states where land originally was sold by the federal government.

Final Accounting: A set of papers in a probate file that outline the complete payment of bills and receipt of payments for an estate.

Genealogy: A study of the family. It identifies ancestors and their information.

Grantee: Purchaser of property.

Grantor: Seller of property.

Hidden Source: A source of information you might not automatically think of when you search for family records.

Historical Context: For family history, historical context is placing a person into a specific era or time period, to view their lives and decisions based on the time in which they lived.

Home Source: A home source is any item or document that will provide facts on people in our family.

Identification Clues: In the context of ephemera, this would include names of individuals along with age(s), date(s) and location(s) that have been handwritten or typewritten onto the ephemera piece.

Immigrant: An individual who comes from one place to another for the purpose of temporary or permanent residence.

Immigration: To enter a place from another for the purpose of temporary or permanent residence.

Indirect Evidence: Information relevant to genealogy research that cannot answer a specific question without other evidence or records.

Individual Deceased Personnel File (IDPF): A file compiled during World War II and beyond which documented the deaths and burials of U.S. soldiers who died while in service to their country. These documents sometimes contain letters from the family; disinterment records; service records; detailed cause of death; and health or state of the body information. (See Burial File)

Intestate: When someone dies without a will.

Interment: The location where a person will be laid to rest or buried.

Inventory: Detailed list of articles of property and their actual or estimated value.

Journal: A diary or notebook or other book in which to record your thoughts.

Letters of Administration: Document issued by the probate court to an individual authorizing them to settle the estate of one who dies intestate.

Letters Testamentary: Document issued to the executor of an estate giving authority to settle the estate of one who died testate.

Maiden Name: A woman's surname, or last name, prior to marriage.

Map: Representation of an area of land or sea showing physical features such as cities, roads, mountains, etc.

Marriage License: An official document issued to a couple so they may be married.

Maternal: Related through the mother's line.

Memorabilia: Items collected and kept because of personal or historical significance.

Migration: The movement of individuals or families from one locale to another.

Military Records: A set of records compiled by the U.S. government regarding an individual's enlistment, service and discharge from the armed forces.

Mortgage: A conditional transfer of a legal title to a piece of property as security for a debt.

Naturalization: A sworn statement, given in court, made by an alien in which he renounces his allegiance to his country of origin and swears allegiance to the United States.

Obituary: A notice of someone's death that usually contains a little biographical information about them.

Occupation: A job.

Original Source: Material that has been unaltered and remains in its original form.

Passport Application: An application to travel outside the country.

Paternal: Related through the father's line.

Pedigree Chart: A chart outlining the ancestors of an individual.

Pension File: File containing documents pertaining to a set fee paid to a U.S. armed forces veteran for past service to the government. These records sometimes contain service information; birth, marriage and death records; family information; and health information.

Photograph: An image made using a camera.

Port of Entry: The port or city where a ship docked and immigrants entered the United States.

Primary Source: A piece of evidence from the past that was created during the event.

Probate: Legal process of settling an estate.

Proof: Evidence or argument establishing or helping to establish a fact or truth of a statement.

Proof of Heirship: Testimony documenting the relationships of heirs listed in a probate file to the deceased.

Quitclaim Deed: A deed by which the person releases all title and claim to a piece of property.

Receipt: Written acknowledgment of receiving something.

Repository: A place or building where things are or may be stored.

Research Log: A worksheet that tracks the genealogical sources you have checked, where you found them, what your comments are about the source, and information you discovered.

Research Notes: Notes created during the research process in the form of written comments using photocopies, abstracts, extracts, transcriptions, and translations.

Research Plan: A plan you create to help you (possibly) solve a genealogical problem. Strategically outlines what you know, what you want to know, where you might be able to find it, and how you will go about implementing this plan.

Scrapbook: A blank book in which documents, photographs, clippings, and ephemera are combined.

Secondary Source: Sources created after an event by people who do not have firsthand knowledge of the event.

Ship Manifest (Passenger List): An official list of all individuals on a given voyage. Information may include name; age; occupation; relative's information; country of origin; town of origin; and physical description.

Social History: The study of the everyday lives of ordinary people.

Source: People, documents, artifacts, and print or digital materials.

Special Collection: Collection of rare manuscripts, books, and other materials that is stored in special rooms to preserve the materials in a library or archive.

Stable: To keep something safe and secure to prevent it from being damaged or destroyed.
State Bonus Applications: Application files for payments of a bonus to the soldier or his beneficiary after World War I and World War II. These records are typically held in State Archives.

State-Land States: A group of twenty states where land originally was sold by the colonial or state government.

Steerage: The lowest part of the ship where tickets were least expensive.

Tax Rolls/Records: Records held by the city and/or county and state which assess the taxes on real and personal property.

Testate: When someone dies with a will.

Timeline: The passage of time represented graphically.

Tradition: The handing down of statements, beliefs, legends, customs, information, etc., from generation to generation, especially by word of mouth or by practice.

Transcribe: In the context of ephemera, to make a written or typewritten copy of all handwritten and typewritten messages and/or notes found on both the front and back of a piece of ephemera.

Trust Deed: A deed where the title is placed in trust to many people (trustees) to secure the payment of the mortgage.

Vital Records: Governmental records on life events such as birth certificates, marriage licenses, and death certificates.

Warranty Deed: The grantor warrants the deed is good and should the title become faulty, the grantor can be sued.

Will: Document in which a Testator disburses his estate, both real and personal property.

About the Author

Jennifer Holik is a genealogical research professional and the owner of Generations. She has a BA in History from Missouri University of Science and Technology.

Jennifer has over sixteen years of research and writing experience and writes several blogs including Kids' Genealogy, Chicago Family History and Family History Research. She has authored articles for local and national genealogical publications. She is a freelance writer for Examiner.com's Chicago Genealogy column. Her book, To Soar with the Tigers, originally written for adults, will be released in juvenile form by early 2013.

Jennifer also lectures in the Chicagoland area on using technology with genealogy and finishing the stories of your military ancestors.

Generations provides top-notch services in the following areas:
- Research and analysis
- Complete house histories
- Document retrieval
- Photography
- Probate work
- Articles for magazines, journals, newsletters, newspapers, and blogs
- Lectures
- Education
- Social Media

Jennifer is a member in good standing of the following local and national organizations:
- Association of Professional Genealogists
- Czech and Slovak American Genealogy Society of Illinois
- DuPage County Genealogical Society (Social Media)
- Federation of Genealogical Societies
- Genealogical Speakers Guild
- Illinois State Genealogical Society (Director)
- International Society of Family History Writers and Editors
- Missouri State Genealogical Society
- National Genealogical Society
- Webster County Missouri Historical Society

Learn more about Generations by visiting http://generationsbiz.com.

Contact the author at jenniferholik@generationsbiz.com

About the Cover Designer

Sarah Sucansky is a freelance graphic designer / art director living near Minneapolis, MN.

About the Editor

Stephanie Pitcher Fishman is a freelance writer and editor, genealogical researcher, and life-long learner. As a homeschooling wife and mother, Stephanie has been involved in the homeschool community through both her personal and professional endeavors since 2000. She is currently the Office Manager for The HomeScholar, helping parents homeschool through high school (http://www.thehomescholar.com).

A genealogical researcher since 1998, Stephanie also writes the Columbus Genealogy column at Examiner.com. She is active in both local and national genealogical societies. She specializes in Midwestern and Southeastern United States family history research, specifically within Ohio and Georgia. Ms. Fishman is pursuing a certificate in Genealogical Studies - American Records through the National Institute for Genealogical Studies and is a member of ProGen 15. You can learn more about her research, writing, and editing services at Corn and Cotton: My Family's Story (http://www.cornandcotton.com).

About the Contributors

Shelley Bishop was fascinated by her grandmother's family stories long before she began doing genealogical research in 2002. Her passion led her to become a professional family history researcher and writer. She has a B.A. in English from Maryville College in Tennessee, and worked for *The Columbus Dispatch* in Ohio for many years.

Once she began sharing her personal discoveries on her blog, *A Sense of Family* (http://www.asenseoffamily.com), Shelley recognized the many ways that modern genealogy builds connections, support, and understanding between people. With her business, Buckeye Family Trees (http://buckeyefamilytrees.com), Shelley specializes in researching and writing about Ohio ancestors. Her services include ancestor and family biographies, family history charts, Union Civil War research, and lineage society applications.

Shelley is a member of the Association of Professional Genealogists, the Daughters of the American Revolution, and several Ohio Genealogical Society lineage groups. She has completed the National Genealogical Society's American Genealogy course of study, and is an active volunteer with local societies and Palatines to America, a German genealogy organization.

Laura Cosgrove Lorenzana is a Consulting Archivist, Genealogist, and writer. A trip to the Louvre Museum in Paris changed the direction of her life and led her to the University of Illinois at Chicago where she earned a BA in Art History with a Certificate in Museum Studies. Since 2006, she's worked as a Consulting Archivist in a wide variety of archives from Shure, Inc. to the Union League Club of Chicago. It was there that Laura's interest in genealogy was resurrected as she assisted researchers in their efforts to locate information about their relatives in the ULCC's collection.

A chance encounter on Twitter connected Laura with Jennifer Holik. It was through Jennifer that Laura renewed her own genealogical research and began her blog, The Last Leaf On This Branch (http://thelastleafonthisbranch.blogspot.com/). Laura's passion for Archives and Genealogy have combined and through her business From Roots to Leaves (http://www.fromrootstoleaves.com), she provide genealogical and personal archival services to those interested in ensuring their long hours of diligent research and lovingly collected family treasures are not lost. She is available for workshops and presentations to groups both small and large.

Laura is a member of the Daughters of the American Revolution, Society of American Archivists, National Genealogical Society, Association of Professional Genealogists, and National Trust for Historic Preservation. Laura enjoys a wide array of other interests including paleography, languages, travel, great food, a wonderful cup of coffee, and stimulating conversation.

Terri O'Connell is travel professional who has been involved with genealogy since 1999. A short unexpected illness claimed the life of her grandfather and left her with many unanswered questions about his family. Through the years, she has had many great discoveries in this family and her other lines as well. Relating travel to genealogy is second nature, we all want to see where our ancestors came from and experience a part of their life.

You may find more about Terri, her genealogy research and travel business through the following websites:

O'Connell Travel	http://www.oconnelltravel.com
Finding Our Ancestors Blog	http://www.findingourancestors.net/what-we-do.html
Researching O'Connells	www.researchingoconnells.wordpress.com
Examiner.com Chicago Travel Chanel	
	http://www.examiner.com/travel-in-chicago/terri-o-connell
Terri's Travel Blog	http://www.myfamilyexcursions.blogspot.com

Caroline M. Pointer is a genealogist, a family historian, a writer, and an author of three main blogs. She has been blogging stories about her ancestors since 2009 on Family Stories. Additionally, she has been having epic results combining genealogy, technology, tutorials, and reviews on her blog 4YourFamilyStory.com. Earlier this year she launched her newest blog creation, BloggingGenealogy.com, to show genealogists, genealogical societies, and professional genealogists how to achieve their blogging and social media goals.

When she is not blogging about dead people; showing others how to use technology to find dead people; or showing others how to blog about dead people more effectively, Caroline can usually be found in an antique store searching for papers, letters, post cards, tickets, photos, books, etc. once owned by dead people because she fancies herself an Ephemera Rescuer and Whisperer. She can be reached at CMPointer@gmail.com .

Books Available from Generations

Paperback available through CreateSpace.

PDFs and PowerPoints available through Generations Store: http://www.e-junkie.com/generations

Branching Out: Genealogy for 1st – 3rd Grade Students Lessons 1-15
https://www.createspace.com/3771098

Branching Out: Genealogy for 1st – 3rd Grade Students Lessons 16-30
https://www.createspace.com/3802448

Branching Out: Genealogy for 4th – 8th Grade Students Lessons 1-15
https://www.createspace.com/3802436

Branching Out: Genealogy for 4th – 8th Grade Students Lessons 16-30
https://www.createspace.com/3802450

Branching Out: Genealogy for High School Students Lessons 1-15
https://www.createspace.com/3802442

Branching Out: Genealogy for High School Students Lessons 16-30
https://www.createspace.com/3802451

Engaging the Next Generation: A Guide for Genealogical Societies and Libraries
Coming May 2012

Watch for a series of Branching Out Teacher books coming Fall 2012!

To Soar with the Tigers
Signed hardcover copies available for purchase on Generations website http://generationsbiz.com
$25 + $5 to ship

Paperback available through CreateSpace
https://www.createspace.com/3549200
$12.99

EPub format available on Lulu.com, Barnes and Noble's Nook and Amazon's Kindle

Genealogy Tip Sheets

Using Excel for Genealogical Research
EPub format available on Lulu.com, Barnes and Noble's Nook and Amazon's Kindle

Locating Chicago Property Records
EPub format available on Lulu.com, Barnes and Noble's Nook and Amazon's Kindle

Quick Guide to Locating World War I Records
EPub format available on Lulu.com, Barnes and Noble's Nook and Amazon's Kindle